# Beyond the Polls

# Beyond The Polls

## Political Ideology and its Correlates

Gerald Kent Hikel
Yale University

**Lexington Books**
D.C. Heath and Company
Lexington, Massachusetts
Toronto          London

Library of Congress Cataloging in Publication Data

Hikel, Gerald Kent.
  Beyond the Polls.

  Bibliography: p.
    1. Right and left (Political science)  2. Ideology.  3. Public opinion—
Detroit metropolitan area.  I. Title.
JF2049.H54           301.15'43'329              73-7974
ISBN 0-669-89284-X

Published simultaneously in Canada.

Printed in the United States of America.

International Standard Book Number: 0-669-89284-X

Library of Congress Catalog Card Number: 73-7974

To my wife, Jane,
and children,
Virginia and Bonnie Jane

# Contents

viii

# Acknowledgments

It is probably more appropriate than is usually the case for me to express my appreciation to a large number of colleagues and friends. First of all, my research was supported by a National Institute of Mental Health Fellowship administered through the Center for Research on Social Organization of the University of Michigan. In addition, Michigan's Department of Sociology allocated considerable computer funds for the research.

Thanks most certainly go to Professors Howard Schuman and Irwin Katz, faculty investigators of Detroit Area Study 1968-1969, for supervising the collection of the data presented herein. And I am also grateful to student investigators in Sociology 501 and 512-513, whose efforts were invaluable in formulation of the survey, and collection and analysis of the data. To Professor James C. Lingoes of the Department of Psychology and the Computing Center, who has both made the Guttman/Lingoes nonmetric technique computer series available, and greatly aided my understanding of the applications of smallest space techniques, I express my gratitude. Also I am thankful to Professor Edward O. Laumann, who first introduced me to smallest space analysis when I served as his research assistant. Much of his work using nonmetric techniques has provided guidelines for this research.

Professors Walter D. Connor, Philip E. Converse, Samuel J. Eldersveld, Daniel Katz, Albert J. Reiss, Jr., and David R. Segal have contributed far beyond their role as critics of this research in its earlier form as the author's doctoral thesis. Each person has through his work and our association stimulated and enlightened my interdisciplinary approach to the political system. I especially wish to acknowledge my considerable debt to David R. Segal. He reviewed my entire manuscript and suggested substantial improvements, particularly in Chapter 5.

Professor Milton Rokeach of Washington State University's Department of Sociology has corresponded with me at various stages of this research and provided helpful suggestions as well as made much of his previously unpublished work available to me.

For whatever inadequacies are apparent I must accept blame, and trust that future research will be of benefit. My only desire is for this investigation to add an extra stone in the building of political sociology.

Finally, my colleague and brother, Ronald Salem Hikel, presently at the Department of Political Science of the University of Winnipeg, has, based on his considerable experience, given me valuable insights into the nature of our political system. My wife, Jane, formerly Senior Secretary at the Center for Research on Social Organization of the University of Michigan, in addition to her exceptional typing skills, has contributed to the development of these ideas as well as been a constant motivating force.

**G.K.H.**

May 1973
New Haven, Connecticut

# List of Tables

# List of Figures

# Beyond the Polls

# 1

## The Structure of Political Belief Systems

### Introduction

This research addresses itself to the political belief systems of the electorate in the Detroit metropolitan area. Our central objective is to develop a framework for dealing with beliefs that allows us to treat the *structure* of mass belief systems. We will ask, so far as possible, in what structural ways do belief systems differ from one another, and what structural properties do all belief systems have in common? Campbell et al. (1960) found familiarity with issues to be unevenly distributed across the electorate. Showing again that attitudinal resources are not randomly distributed across the population, Converse (1964) finds the electorate to fall into five levels of conceptualization [1] It is determined that only a tiny fraction of the electorate are constrained in their political attitudes by an "overriding" ideology.

As a result of the definition of ideology by the characteristics of the liberalism-conservatism continuum, the vast majority of voters are seen to hold "unstructured" beliefs. The conceptualization of political beliefs in terms of the liberalism-conservatism dimension involves implicitly a *balance theory* model. Where belief elements are consistent the system is balanced; inconsistent beliefs lead to an imbalance. Consistency itself is based on psychological constraints. Those members of our political system who are elites "have *experienced* them [the total shapes of belief systems] as logically constrained clusters of ideas within which one part necessarily follows from another" (Converse, 1964:211).

We believe that a major weakness of present theory is a lack of understanding of the conditions under which political beliefs cluster. Beliefs may show relationships which fall beyond the scope of balance theory. Perhaps a more adequate view of belief systems is provided by Kurt Lewin's (1951) field theory. The basic advantage of a field theory perspective is that it offers a broader grasp of the possible interrelationships among beliefs, independent of temporal and logical constraints (Wilker and Milbrath, 1970).

Although Converse does not neglect a consideration of other bases of constraint, some investigators do treat his findings in isolation. In one recently published article the author advances his suggestion that "political attitudes are an elite phenomenon. Most people do not have political attitudes" (Hennessy, 1970:463).

We wish, therefore, to explore the bases other than liberalism-conservatism which nourish belief structures. We see any theoretical approach to the analysis

1

of beliefs which completely neglects alternative dimensions as untenable. The meaningfulness of our approach is highlighted by the often documented stability of partisan loyalties. The very existence, or more precisely, persistence, of stable partisan identification patterns among the electorate suggests stable belief systems. Wilker and Milbrath (1970:480) suggest that "it is difficult to conceive of stable behavior without some kind of stable belief structure lying behind that behavior." For these scholars (1970:480-481) as well as for us, "The fact that ideological belief systems are rarely found in the mass public does not lead to the conclusion that ordinary people do not have belief systems that are relevant for understanding their political behavior."

All political belief systems are not necessarily ideological (Sartori, 1969:400). Since evidence shows that the majority of citizens are not policy oriented in their political attitudes, we should expect belief systems to be structured on other bases. Katz (1960:187) shows how voting behavior is largely motivated by the symbolic expression of one's *values*. In a similar vein, Wilker and Milbrath (1970:488) point out that, "Much of the political activity of ordinary citizens involves the pursuit of expressive goals." Wilker and Milbrath argue that "expressive purposes" underline the structure of belief systems in the mass public, and therefore it is to the purposes of political action which we must turn for an understanding of political belief systems. Although Wilker and Milbrath do not use the term "value," we can reasonably see the concepts of goal or purpose and value as synonymous.

The question is not then, does the mass public have structured beliefs but rather, what are the motivational bases for political activity? Our approach, though, must first of all involve testing Converse's finding that only a minority of the electorate are ideologues as defined by the liberalism-conservatism dimension.[2] Later we will consider to what extent by expanding our consideration of the bases of constraint among beliefs the entire electorate can be included in the discussion of belief structures.

Throughout this investigation the issues of partisanship and ideology are intertwined. Our instruments enable us to differentiate among partisans and as well as among ideological positions. Thus, certain hypotheses about the nature of both partisans and ideologues will be tested. Most notably in regard to partisanship, we will consider the portrayal of Independents as the least likely to be politically aware. In addition, our line of analysis will include a consideration of social-psychological characteristics, so that we will associate attitudinal as well as psychological concerns with partisanship and ideology. Having already mentioned the particular importance of a discussion of values for understanding the structure of belief systems, we will weave into the development of our analysis a theory about the role of political values in its implications for the integration of the electorate's beliefs within the political system.

Finally, the order of investigation suggests that a limited discussion of how the political system plays a role in structuring the belief systems of the electorate be included. One fairly common theme argues for the relevance of political information to the stratification of belief strata. As Converse (1964:248) points out, "ideological constraints in belief systems decline with decreasing information. . . ." The limited extent to which the mass public feels ideological constraints in its belief systems depends in part upon the activities of the political elite. As Sartori (1969:408) puts it, borrowing on Lane's (1962) distinction, "the ideologic or pragmatic qualification of mass publics—of the *latent* beliefs—is largely decided by the *forensic* beliefs, by the elite belief system to which mass publics are exposed."

In the last analysis it is clear that without efforts to investigate the configuration of attitudes and psychological orientations we cannot hope to accurately understand the reality of the nature of political man. The correlations between attitude items can be translated into a geometric relationship, so as to yield a more comprehensive picture of the empirical patterns. We hope to clarify certain problems that unfortunately often remain only implicit or ambiguous in the literature on political sociology.[3]

## The Liberalism-Conservatism Continuum

Major political realignments have been rare in American history. The last is often said to have occurred during the thirties when Franklin D. Roosevelt molded a coalition of workers, Southerners, blacks, urbanites, and intellectuals into the majority party of the country. From that time until very recently, the basic outlines of American political conflict remained amazingly consistent with little change in the broad political strategies of the national parties. Some scholars argue that in 1968 the American polity entered a new phase of realignment. While some body of political theory and evidence supports this view, it is too early at this writing to determine whether the elections of 1968 and 1972 represent a realignment of the normal vote of the American electorate or are merely deviations from this vote.

The political issues that arose out of the Depression and the New Deal, for over 30 years, gave structure to the American political landscape. The country has followed a foreign policy that is largely bipartisan and a domestic policy that has revolved around the issues of welfare and the role of government in the nation's economy. The stability of the political system has prompted social scientists to adopt the left-right or liberal-conservative spectrum as a descriptive mechanism along which party competition and voter affiliation in the United States could be determined. Setting aside the boundaries of the American political system, Stokes (1966) suggests that the use of spatial ideas to interpret party competition is a universal phenomenon of modern politics.

Social scientists have long been accustomed to conceiving of variations in political orientation as being ordered along a *single liberalism-conservatism continuum.* Recently there have been a considerable number of criticisms of this nearly ubiquitous unidimensional approach, as well as several attempts to present alternative models (Axelrod, 1967; Converse, 1966; Ladd, 1969; Stokes, 1966). Shils (1954) has suggested that this construct does not represent political reality in the twentieth century, and Lipset (1968) argues that if it is to be used, it must at least be defined in terms of general policy arenas, i.e., social welfare and civil liberties. Efforts by the staff of the Survey Research Center at the University of Michigan to define the structure of political attitudes have gone far toward the definition of such attitudes in terms of specific policy areas (see, for example, Campbell et al., 1960). Reanalysis of Survey Research Center data, however, suggests that there is indeed a liberalism-conservatism dimension underlying, and cutting across, issue areas (cf. Segal and Smith, 1970), and La Ponce's (1970) success in using this dimension with college samples suggests that it is indeed meaningful, at least to educated subgroups. Moreover, Rice's (1928:275) earlier research indicates that for educated populations the distribution of this dimension may indeed be bell shaped. We shall, therefore, focus on this construct in our own research.

One critical area in which we differ with previous researchers is in our rejection of their assumption that the structure of ideology is *unidimensional.* Rather, we propose that these researchers are looking at only one of several alternative bases of the structure of beliefs. In this investigation, we are concerned with how people relate to the two major American political parties, specifically with the extent to which people see themselves as more liberal than, or more conservative than, these parties. Linked with this concern is our interest in how individual positions and strength of party support correlate. From these data on individual perspectives we shall be able to draw inferences regarding the degree to which there is consensus on the relative ideological positions of the parties. In adopting this approach we are attending to the criticisms raised by Stokes (1966) and by Buchanan and Tullock (1965) regarding the assumption of unidimensionality.

That there is yet little consensus about the structure of belief systems is substantiated by the existence of a considerable number of different formal models. As Levinson suggests: "It would be helpful . . . if the purely political meaning of the terms 'conservative' and 'radical' were clearly defined and widely agreed upon" (Levinson, 1968:22). Unfortunately, most authors facing the challenge of the definition of liberalism-conservatism admit that it is not their purpose to resolve the question of its real definition. Thus the definitions that have been offered are rarely comprehensive, and too often we find the commentators presenting ideas about liberalism-conservatism or alternative dimensions, and not directly addressing the problematic nature of belief systems.

Most current interpretations of the organization of attitudes are implicitly underlined by the assumption of a liberalism-conservatism dimension. This approach is still common in spite of Converse's (1964) finding that the vast majority of citizens cannot articulate their beliefs on this dimension. One of our major concerns is a consideration of whether variations in electoral behavior can indeed be meaningfully ordered along a single dimension. To meet this objective we will propose a factor that limits the usefulness of the conventional left-right dimension.

*Liberalism-Conservatism: A Theoretical Weakness*

Although one looks in vain for an analysis of the precise number of defining attributes of liberalism-conservatism, two attributes are most obvious. The liberalism-conservatism concept combines both *stylistic* and *ideological* attributes. The stylistic attribute defines voters in terms of how they relate to the status quo; the ideological attribute involves the more specific content of the belief system. Levinson (1968) touches on both aspects when he equates conservatism and liberalism with Right and Left and then defines the Right as supporting the status quo, tradition, stability, and a hierarchical social order, and the Left as critical of the status quo and seeking instead social and economic equality.

As Milbrath (1965:7) writes, "[the] liberal-conservative contention about what should be done with the status quo is a familiar theme through many centuries of political writing." Milbrath points out the usefulness of considering the ideological attribute as well as the stylistic when he says that many attitudes cannot be fitted into this general liberal-conservative dimension; "they are even more specific as to setting and time, and therefore, are even more difficult to summarize" (Milbrath, 1965:7). The ideological attribute is based on the particular "agenda of politics," i.e., the dominant issues, which change periodically.

A liberal supports change in the status quo in order to achieve a more popular or equal distribution of some important social value: a higher standard of living, more and better public education, assurance of adequate health care, etc. (Ladd, 1970:203). If, as McClosky (1958) suggests, some personalities are inclined in a conservative direction, we should find conservatives who support the status quo *independently* of ideological considerations. This suggests that the ideological and stylistic aspects of a political philosophy vary independently. For example, a Communist, while strongly favoring social and economic equality, might be reactionary in his perception of the status quo once the revolution is completed. On the other hand, Lenin himself, while committed ideologically to the value of equality, had a very elitist conception of the Communist (Sabine, 1953). As we discuss later, the value of equality is of central concern when one examines political belief systems.

"Presumably, persons inclined either liberally or conservatively would adopt a corresponding position with respect to the status quo no matter what setting or era they lived in" (Milbrath, 1965:7). If one knew who the status-changers and status-defenders were, one could presumably predict to their partisan identification if not to their specific issue orientations—the changers tending to support a more leftist, and the defenders to choose a more rightist party. One possibility is that the liberalism-conservatism concept is adequate when it comes to predicting to the stylistic attribute for the mass public, and to the ideological attribute for the more aware, but not vice versa. On face we may find that the stylistic aspect is as adequate a predictor for nonideologues, as the ideological aspect is in predicting to ideologues. Extending this line of reasoning, the liberalism-conservatism dimension is in one sense anchored by time, yet in another sense is not.

The most general meaning of the terms liberal and conservative—the stylistic—transcends time. There are always conservatives, those who support the status quo, and liberals, who oppose it. In this broad usage, all men are either more or less conservative or more or less liberal. To the extent that the actors use extreme means to preserve the status quo we may speak of a reactionary segment, or to change the status quo we may speak of a revolutionary segment.

Of course there are periodic shifts in the political spectrum, as the apparent decrease in the proportion of Republicans in the electorate documents. However there is always by definition a status quo, and we are prepared to argue that those who support the status quo (and similarly those who reject it) are likely to have characteristics that transcend temporal shifts in specific issue orientation. In at least one sense the questions we are investigating transcend the temporal dimension. Thus the absence of longitudinal measures of issue orientation is somewhat less of a limitation. Our instruments may allow us to measure the orientation of individual respondents toward the political system somewhat independently of the content of these beliefs.

**The Data Base**

These concerns were explored using data collected by the Detroit Area Survey, University of Michigan, during the spring and summer of 1969. A multistage probability sample of dwelling units in the Detroit Metropolitan area was drawn.[4] The geographical area used for this study was that part of Detroit tracted in 1950, plus some small additions to include recent suburban population growth. The sample area included 90 percent of the population of Wayne, Macomb and Oakland Counties, minus the City of Pontiac and outlying semirural areas. This area is consistent with several previous Detroit Area Study surveys.

Only dwelling units defined by the 1950 Census were sampled. Institutions, boarding houses, and dormitories were excluded, except insofar as they contained a dwelling unit. Within each dwelling unit having one or more eligible respondents, the head or wife was drawn at random for an interview. When only the household head was present, he or she was always interviewed. Only whites were interviewed because of the general subject matter—white racial attitudes—of the study. The target population of individuals living in dwelling units within the geographical area were selected if they met all the following criteria: white, 69 years of age or younger, head of house, or spouse of head. The effect of the restrictions was to exclude blacks, dwelling units occupied by persons 70 years old and up, children, and some adults such as dependent parents and unrelated individuals living with a head.

Utilizing a sampling fraction of 1/900, blocks were selected with a probability proportional to the estimated number of dwelling units in them. Within each selected block, segments of expected size (six dwelling units) were selected with equal probability, such that the segments were on opposite sides of the block. Alterations in the sampling procedure occurred when the actual number of dwelling units on the block was greater or less than expected. Such segments were selected to test certain hypotheses about ecological and neighborhood effects on respondents. This procedure did not alter the probability of a dwelling unit's being included in the sample, each dwelling unit having an equal probability of being drawn.

The sample was divided into two nearly equal parts, half being assigned to Detroit Area Study student interviewers, and the other half to professional interviewers of the University of Michigan's Survey Research Center. The final sample contained 640 interviews, representing 76 percent of the eligible households sampled. This sample size is considerably less than the goal of 700 interviews. Sixteen percent of the households refused interviews, and 8 percent were not completed because the respondent was not found at home or for other reasons. The low response rate of 76 percent—lowest in the eighteen-year history of Detroit Area Study—indicates that certain precautions must be taken in analyzing the 1969 Detroit Area Study findings. The sample could be biased by the possible exclusion of particular social types.

The major reason for the low response rate is, of course, the proportion of refusals. Survey research organizations have indicated a long run decline in response rates, but the 1969 rate is particularly low.[5] It might be suggested that the topic of racial attitudes, which was the primary concern of this survey, is a sensitive one from which some potential respondents would withdraw. However, interviewers are instructed not to inform the respondent as to the specific topic until the interview is in progress, and it is unusual for an interview to be ended before completion.

One other interesting possibility is related to the selection of the sample. Interviewers were assigned clusters within a block, and interviewing of the respondents within a cluster was most typically extended over several days. Thus, negative opinions about the interviewers or the interview could have been circulated from neighbor to neighbor. And of course in 1969 the University of

Michigan and student interviewers might have symbolized objectionable protest activities to a large percentage of those who refused interviews.[6] The possible systematic exclusion of such respondents raises a question about reliability that should be of concern to all survey research organizations. For each dwelling unit selected a cover sheet was prepared (see Appendix A). Therefore, limited information, primarily ecological data, is available on noninterviews. The data indicate that refusals tend to come from the inner city area. Given the somewhat greater reluctance to interact with strangers in the inner city, this is not a particularly surprising finding.

*Detroit Area Data vs. National Data*

Our data should allow us to make inferences about the Detroit Area with a reasonable degree of confidence. Can our data be used to draw conclusions about the American electorate? Assuredly only to the extent that our data are representative may the data be applicable to a broader sphere of interest.

We turned for clarification of the question of representativeness to the Survey Research Center's 1968 Election Study. The sample selection criteria are quite similar, both being cluster samples. Moreover, the surveys were conducted within seven to ten months of one another. We feel, therefore, that the Survey Research Center's study permits us to make the necessary comparisons. Our percent comparisons on social background variables between the Detroit Area Study sample and that of the Survey Research Center are based on 640 Detroit area respondents (not weighted) and 1,673 Survey Research Center respondents (weighted = 3,101). Where the total percentage does not equal 100, there are missing data (see Table 1-1).

Analysis of the age distribution of the two samples shows our Detroit Area sample to be considerably younger. This difference is accounted for by the fact that in our sample the actual age boundaries are 18-69 years, whereas the Survey Research Center conducted interviews of the entire voting age population. There are no significant differences by age in decades between the samples but 10 percent of the Survey Research Center's sample is above age 70. This difference might suggest that the national sample be somewhat more inclined toward the Republican Party (see Campbell et al., 1960: 155). There is in fact only a slightly greater percentage of respondents in the national sample who are Republican.

The Independents in the Detroit sample seem to benefit from the somewhat younger age distribution, there being 2 percent more in our sample than nationally. The Democrat percentage is nearly identical. The age distribution also suggests that we could expect to find more widowed among the national sample, and the national sample is in fact found to include twice as many widowed respondents.

Not only is there a greater percentage of widowed among the national sample, but a somewhat greater percentage of single adults as well. Some of these may

**Table 1-1**

**Percent Distribution by Background Factors of Detroit Area and National Samples**

| | | Detroit (N = 640) (Percent) | National (N = 3,101) (Percent) |
|---|---|---|---|
| Age | Less than 30 years | 21.6 | 18.3 |
| Groups | 30 - 50 years | 44.6 | 40.2 |
| | Above 50 years | 33.7 | 41.0 |
| | Total | 99.9 | 99.9 |
| Party | Republican | 22.2 | 24.2 |
| Affiliation | Democrat | 44.5 | 44.9 |
| | Independent | 31.1 | 29.1 |
| | Total | 97.8 | 98.2 |
| Marital | Single | 6.7 | 8.8 |
| Status | Married | 79.5 | 70.6 |
| | Divorced | 5.0 | 5.1 |
| | Separated | 2.2 | 2.8 |
| | Widowed | 6.6 | 12.6 |
| | Total | 100.0 | 99.9 |
| Sex | Male | 47.5 | 43.7 |
| | Female | 52.5 | 56.3 |
| | Total | 100.0 | 100.0 |
| Years of | Some high school or less | 35.0 | 39.8 |
| Education | High School | 36.2 | 32.0 |
| | Some College + | 28.8 | 27.1 |
| | Total | 100.0 | 100.0 |
| Family | Under $4,000 | 7.0 | 22.9 |
| Income | $4,000 - 7,999 | 15.8 | 30.8 |
| | $8,000 - 11,999 | 35.7 | 23.2 |
| | $12,000 - 19,999 | 30.5 | 14.9 |
| | Over $20,000 | 7.0 | 5.1 |
| | Total | 96.0 | 96.9 |
| Occupation | Professional, technical and managerial | 29.5 | 28.1 |
| | Clerical and Sales | 14.2 | 10.9 |
| | Craftsman | 24.8 | 18.2 |
| | Operatives | 19.5 | 15.2 |
| | Service workers and laborers | 8.9 | 15.6 |
| | Students, military, housewives, NA | 2.9 | 11.9 |
| | Total | 99.8 | 99.9 |

**Table 1-1**

|  |  | Detroit (N = 640) (Percent) | National (N = 3,101) (Percent) |
|---|---|---|---|
| Religion | Protestant | 48.5 | 70.5 |
|  | Catholic | 43.2 | 21.9 |
|  | Jew | 1.7 | 2.7 |
|  | Total | 93.4 | 95.1 |

perhaps be spinsters. The latter possibility, combined with the fact that women live longer, should hint toward a sex ratio more strongly favoring females in the national sample. There is a greater percentage of females over males in the national sample. So far the background variables reveal considerable similarity once the age distributions of the interviewed are taken into account.

Education of respondents is also quite similar across the Detroit Area and national data. Although the Detroit Area sample, representing an urban population, is somewhat more highly educated, the differences in the distributions might reflect in part the above average quality of the Michigan public educational system. The relative youth of the Detroit sample is a more likely explanatory factor here. One might argue, given the difference in education, that a measure of political sophistication would find a slightly higher average level of conceptualization in the Detroit electorate relative to the American electorate.

Family income levels should be higher than the national average in and around the "Motor City." There are considerable differences in family income distributions. The younger Detroit Area sample should include fewer retired respondents living on social security. Since the Detroit Area Study only includes whites, and whites have a lower unemployment rate, here is another factor that could in part account for residents in the Detroit Area sample having higher income levels. The strength of local unions should also be taken into account.

Education probably also enters into the income differences. Occupation should help to clarify the income differentials. Occupational differences seem more moderate than income differences. Those of highest occupational status account for a very similar percentage of each group. If the not applicable (NA) categories were deleted and the percentages were computed, all the differences would lessen, except for the "service and laborer" category where the national sample approaches twice the percentage found among the Detroit Area sample. Surely, the larger percent of students, military personnel, and housewives in the national sample fits into the lower income pattern.

What about the religious factor? The Detroit Area sample has a markedly greater proportion of Catholics, as Table 1-1 shows. The large Polish community, combined with the relatively large numbers of Italians, Irish, and French, probably make up most of the Catholic segment. This does raise an interesting possibility: Are we likely to find an unusually high level of political awareness in an area with high family income, yet low ascribed status as measured by religion? The small percentage of Jews is surprising, inasmuch as the Detroit Area is very urbanized.

Summing up these comparisons between the local and national samples, we can state that the two samples are not particularly comparable. The Detroit sample is a Northern urban sample drawn in an area where labor unions have unusually high political influence. Thus, we must be cautious in making inferences about the American electorate as a whole where income, religious, and other of the factors considered are crucial. Only to the extent that the samples agree with one another are we justified in drawing conclusions for the entire population. On the other hand, knowledge of how the samples differ sensitizes us to certain differences in attitudes and belief system that we might expect, and in this way underline regularities in the relevance of social antecedents for political belief systems. The consideration of such limitations can only add to our understanding.

## The Measurement of the Liberalism-Conservatism Dimension

Positions on the liberalism-conservatism dimension were measured by two questions. All respondents were asked: "Do you think your own views are more liberal or more conservative than those of the Democratic Party generally, or would you say that you're not sure?" and "How about the Republicans? Do you think your own views are generally more liberal or more conservative than those of the Republican Party, or would you say you're not sure?"

On the basis of the above two questions we constructed a measure of ideology that tells us if the respondent perceives the existence of a fundamental liberal-conservative axis, and about the specific manner in which the respondent relates to this continuum. These measures will allow us to compare those who conceive of this continuum with those who do not. Further, we can consider possible variations that occur within the subsegments of the sample who use the liberalism-conservatism construct. In a sense, we defined one distinct segment of the sample for whom the liberalism-conservatism dimension was meaningful. Those who don't view the political parties in liberal-conservative terms come within our scope of investigation as a comparison group.

In spite of certain difficulties of measurement, the respondents generally seem to distribute themselves in the expected fashion.[7] Of our 640 respondents, 260 or slightly more than 40 percent placed themselves on a liberalism-conservatism continuum relative to each of the major parties. As can be seen from Table 1-2, the majority of respondents answering this question did place themselves near the middle of the spectrum—i.e., more conservative than the Democratic

**Table 1-2**

**Positions of Respondents on Liberalism-Conservatism Relative to Democratic and Republican Parties (N=640)**

|  | More Liberal (Percent) | About Same (Percent) | More Conservative (Percent) | Refused D.K., N.A. (Percent) | Total (Percent) |
|---|---|---|---|---|---|
| Republican | 21.7 (53) | 4.7 (12) | 14.2 (35) | 59.4 | 100 |
| Democrat | 11.9 (29) | 4.5 (11) | 24.2 (60) | 59.4 | 100 |

Note: The revised percentages, based on 260 cases for each party, appear in parentheses.

Party, more liberal than the Republican Party. The tendency for the majority of respondents to lean towards the *middle* of the political spectrum is more obvious when the missing data are excluded from the percentage calculations.

One of the questions that concerned us was whether there was consensus among our respondents that the Republican Party was more conservative than the Democratic Party. Of our 640 respondents, 313 placed themselves on the liberalism-conservatism dimension with regard to at least one of the parties. Sixty-three compared themselves to the Republicans but not to the Democrats, 63 to the Democrats but not the Republicans, and 197, or about 31 percent of the total sample, related themselves to both parties. The data collected from these latter respondents are presented in Table 1-3.

The shaded area of Table 1-3 represents those positions that are *logically* possible if it is assumed that the Republicans are more conservative than the Democrats. Ninety-one percent of the respondents appearing in this table fall into these positions, indicating a high level of consensus among those of our respondents who were willing to place themselves on the liberalism-conservatism dimension regarding the relative positions of the major parties.[8] Figure 1-1 presents this distribution graphically. For the 177 people who apply the terms

**Table 1-3**

**Positions on the Liberalism-Conservatism Continuum Relative to Both Parties (N=197)**

|  |  | Republicans | | |
|---|---|---|---|---|
|  |  | More Liberal | About Same (Percent) | More Conservative |
| Democrats | More liberal | 21 | 2 | 5 |
|  | About same | 5 | 1 | 1 |
|  | More conservative | 27 | 8 | 29 |

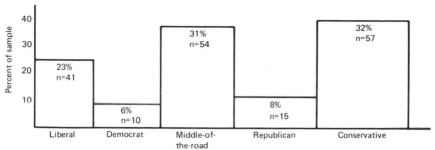

**Figure 1-1.** Distribution of Respondents Who Agreed that the Republican Party Is More Conservative than the Democratic Party (n=177). Note: We define the categories of ideologues as follows: *Liberal:* ideologues more liberal than both parties. *Organizational Democrats:* ideologues more liberal than the Republican party and the same as the Democratic party. *Middle-of-the-roaders:* ideologues more liberal than the Republican party, and more conservative than the Democratic party. *Organizational Republicans:* ideologues more conservative than the Democratic party, and the same as the Republican party. *Conservative:* ideologues more conservative than both parties.

liberal and conservative consistently to themselves and to the two political parties (some 28 percent of our total sample) there is clearly not a normal distribution of political affect. Rather, the distribution is trimodal. Fully 55 percent of these voters see themselves either more conservative or more liberal than both political parties.

The forces of divergence generated by these extreme positions, however, are offset at least to some extent by the 31 percent of this segment of the sample that sees itself more conservative than the Democrats and more liberal than the Republicans. It is notable that only 14 percent of these voters see themselves as occupying the same political position as either of the major parties. Yet, as we discuss in Appendix B, there are certain questions of measurement which caution us as to the accuracy of these results.

Those who employ ideological labels are then a distinct minority. Campbell et al. (1960:249), found 12 percent of their sample to be ideologues or near ideologues, with some 42 percent of the sample responding to nonideological group interests. These levels of conceptualization are derived from information based on extensive questioning of respondents. On the other hand, ours is a measure of the ability to use ideological labels. Fitting our usage of the concept ideology into context with that of Campbell et al., it is immediately apparent that the ability to associate liberalism-conservatism with the major parties involves a less rigorous measurement than interattitude consistency.

There may conceivably have been some upgrading of the level of political conceptualization of the American population in the past decade, or differences between the Detroit and national samples may even be of considerable importance. However, these factors are certainly not enough to justify the conclusion that we are measuring identical constructs. Thus our operationalization of the concept ideology is a less stringent one, and among our concerns we must consider the adequacy of this measure.

# 2

## Ideology and Political Partisanship

### Introduction

We have suggested in the previous chapter that political ideologues in Detroit are in general agreement in placing the Democratic party to the *left* of the Republican party. We now turn to a more intensive exploration of the relationship between partisanship and ideology. Since Independents will be dealt with in a separate chapter, most of this discussion will involve differences among partisans.

The respondents in our sample were asked: "Do you consider yourself a Democrat, a Republican, or what?" People who claim identification with either the Democratic or Republican parties are then asked: "Do you consider yourself a strong (Democrat/Republican) or not a very strong (Democrat/Republican)?" Individuals who declare themselves at the outset to be Independent are asked whether they generally favor the Democratic or Republican party.

The plurality of our sample (44.5 percent) identified themselves as Democrats. Only 22.2 percent called themselves Republicans, while 31.1 percent identified themselves as Independents. Further, only some 2 percent of the sample failed to answer the partisanship question.

The preponderance of Democrats in the sample is not surprising, given the role that labor unions play in Detroit politics. The proportion of Independents in the sample is greater than comparable figures from previous surveys in the Detroit area. It is partly understandable, however, in view of the disruptive effect of the 1968 presidential election on members of the electorate who had affective ties to political parties but were unhappy with the candidate of their particular party (cf. Converse et al., 1969). Indeed, while the 1969 electorate can in no way be viewed as representative of the electorate in all years, it is especially well adapted to our purposes because of the size of the pool of Independents that it allows us to analyze.

The weakening of traditional partisan ties is not only reflected in the increased proportion of Independents in the electorate. As Table 2-1 shows, supporters of both parties were less likely to see themselves as "strong" than as "not strong" supporters of their party, and Independents were most likely to see themselves as leaning toward neither major party. One might reasonably argue then that there has been a considerable transition in political affect away from traditional ties.

**Table 2-1**
**"Strength" and "Leaning" of Political Positions (N=618)**

| | Party Position | | | | | | | |
| --- | --- | --- | --- | --- | --- | --- | --- | --- |
| | Republican | | | Democrat | | | Independent | |
| | Percent | (N) | | Percent | (N) | | Percent | (N) |
| Strong | 36 | (50) | Strong | 38 | (106) | Republican | 20 | (38) |
| Not strong | 64 | (92) | Not strong | 62 | (176) | Democrat | 35 | (67) |
| | | | | | | Neither | 45 | (89) |
| Total | 100 | (142) | | 100 | (282) | | 100 | (194) |

Note: Data on "strength" or "leaning" are missing for eight respondents.

### The Liberalism-Conservatism Dimension
### and Partisanship

Let us now consider how the ability to place oneself on the liberalism conservatism dimension relates to party identification for the total sample. Such is the state of political sociology that no one to our knowledge has dealt with the question of whether Democrats, Republicans, or Independents are more likely to be ideologues. This underscores our concern for an investigation of the Independent.

When comparing the distribution of party affiliation among ideologues and among the total sample, an intriguing finding emerges. Republicans—22 percent of the total sample are proportionately the most likely to be ideologues. They are overrepresented in the ideologue group by some 10 percent, while the Democrats—45 percent of the total sample—are underrepresented by 12 percent. And contrary to the portrayal of Independents as being less likely to be politically sophisticated than partisans (Campbell et al., 1960:143-145; Milbrath, 1965:65-66), our Independents—31 percent of the total sample—reveal a mild overrepresentation of 4 percent. Thus Independents are *not* found to be the least ideological element in the electorate.

Of those who identify themselves as Republicans, 56 (39 percent) of the total of 142 are ideologues. This compares to 31 percent of 199 Independents and 21 percent of 285 Democrats. Thus Republicans are nearly twice as likely as Democrats to be ideologues, and Independents are half again as likely as Democrats to be ideologues.

Table 2-2 presents a seven position measure of party identification by use of liberal and conservative labels. Strong Republicans (52 percent) are by a considerable margin the most likely, and Democrats both strong and weak (21 percent) are the least likely to be ideologues. The Independents of Republican

**Table 2-2**
**Party Identification by Use of Ideological Labels (N=618)**

| | Strong Dem. (106) (Percent) | Weak Dem. (176) (Percent) | Ind. Dem. (67) (Percent) | Ind. (89) (Percent) | Ind. Rep. (38) (Percent) | Weak Rep. (92) (Percent) | Strong Rep. (50) (Percent) |
|---|---|---|---|---|---|---|---|
| | Party Seven-position Identification | | | | | | |
| Ideologue | 21 | 21 | 37 | 22 | 40 | 33 | 52 |
| Inconsistent | 7 | 3 | 3 | 2 | 5 | 0 | 2 |
| Republican | 18 | 8 | 3 | 8 | 5 | 8 | 18 |
| Democrat | 15 | 11 | 12 | 8 | 0 | 8 | 8 |
| Nonideologue | 40 | 57 | 45 | 60 | 50 | 51 | 20 |
| Total | 100 | 100 | 100 | 100 | 100 | 100 | 100 |

Note: We employ the following categories to refer to recognition of the liberalism-conservatism dimension:

*Ideologue*. respondents who place themselves on liberalism-conservatism relative to both parties.
*Inconsistent ideologues:* respondents who don't see Republicans as more conservative than the Democrats.
*Democratic labelers:* respondents who place themselves on liberalism-conservatism relative to the Democratic Party, but not the Republican Party.
*Republican labelers:* respondents who place themselves on liberalism-conservatism relative to the Republican Party, but not the Democratic Party.
*Nonideologues:* respondents who do not place themselves on liberalism-conservatism relative to either party.
Categories (3) and (4) combine to form the one-party labeler category.
For 8 cases the data on strength of affiliation or leaning are missing.

leaning are the second most likely to be ideologues, with the Independents of Democratic leaning and the weak Republicans falling close behind. In considering the likelihood of being a nonideologue, there is little doubt that the main division appears between those who identify themselves as strong Republicans and the rest of the sample.

In Table 2-3 we look only at those Independents who put to use ideological labels. Again, a *trimodal* distribution is obvious. Independents who use ideological labels are about as likely to place themselves to the left of both parties, to the right of both parties, or between both parties.

Moving on to the Republican ideologues, we find the largest group to be the conservatives, followed by the middle-of-the-roaders. For the Democratic ideologues we immediately notice an increase in the number of inconsistent responses.[1] There is then less agreement among Democratic identifiers about the meaning of ideological labels. While there are no Republicans who see themselves occupying the same political position as the Democratic party, two Democrats place themselves in the same position as the Republican party. This incon-

**Table 2-3**
**Position of Respondents on Liberalism-Conservatism Continuum Relative to Both Parties**

| | | | Republican Party | | |
|---|---|---|---|---|---|
| | | | More Liberal | About Same | More Conservative |
| Independents (N=67) | Democratic Party | More liberal | 17 | 3 | 2 |
| | | About same | 2 | 1 | 0 |
| | | More conservative | 18 | 4 | 20 |
| | | | Republican Party | | |
| | | | More Liberal | About Same | More Conservative |
| Republican (N=57) | Democratic Party | More liberal | 7 | 0 | 0 |
| | | About same | 0 | 1 | 0 |
| | | More conservative | 16 | 9 | 24 |
| | | | Republican Party | | |
| | | | More Liberal | About Same | More Conservative |
| Democrats (N=72) | Democratic Party | More liberal | 16 | 1 | 8 |
| | | About same | 8 | 1 | 3 |
| | | More conservative | 20 | 2 | 13 |

sistency, based on only two cases, is divided among those who consider themselves strong and weak Democrats. The largest group of Democratic identifiers are the middle-of-the-roaders, next the liberal and the conservative groups, which are of nearly equal size. Democratic identifiers, a significant minority of whom believe themselves to be more conservative than both parties, appear to be more divided than Republicans in their ideological orientations.

It is interesting that strong Republicans tend to be more conservative than weak Republicans, who are balanced between middle-of-the-roaders and conservatives. On the other hand, strong Democrats tend to be more liberal than weak Democrats, the largest group of whom are middle-of-the-roaders. Among both weak Republicans and Democrats, middle-of-the-roaders are more numerous than among the strong partisans. Thus, strength of affiliation seems to have an impact on an individual's ideological orientation.

In Table 2-4 we consider the relationship between party identification and liberalism-conservatism with regard to a *single party*. Strong Republicans are the most likely to use ideological labels. Some 42 percent of strong Democrats place themselves on the liberalism-conservatism dimension relative to the Democratic

Table 2-4

**Party Affiliation and Position on Liberalism-Conservatism Continuum Relative to the Democratic and Republican Parties (N=618)**

| | Ideological Position Relative to | | | | | | | | | |
| --- | --- | --- | --- | --- | --- | --- | --- | --- | --- | --- |
| | Democratic Party | | | | | Republican Party | | | | |
| Party Position | More Liberal | About Same | More Conservative | Don't Know | Total (Percent) | More Liberal | About Same | More Conservative | Don't Know | Total (Percent) |
| Strong Democrat (N=106) | 17 | 16 | 9 | 58 | 100 | 29 | 2 | 13 | 56 | 100 |
| Weak Democrat (N=176) | 12 | 4 | 20 | 64 | 100 | 19 | 1 | 12 | 68 | 100 |
| Independent Democrat (N=67) | 10 | 3 | 37 | 50 | 100 | 22 | 4 | 15 | 59 | 100 |
| Independent (N=89) | 16 | 1 | 16 | 67 | 100 | 22 | 3 | 10 | 66 | 100 |
| Independent Republican (N=38) | 10 | 3 | 32 | 55 | 100 | 21 | 13 | 16 | 50 | 100 |
| Weak Republican (N=92) | 6 | 0 | 34 | 60 | 100 | 22 | 3 | 16 | 59 | 100 |
| Strong Republican (N=50) | 6 | 2 | 54 | 38 | 100 | 18 | 24 | 30 | 28 | 100 |

Note: Data on partisanship are missing for 14 respondents and on strength or leaning for 8 respondents.

party, and 44 percent place themselves relative to the Republican party. On the other hand, the majority of strong Republicans—62 percent relative to the Democratic party and 72 percent relative to the Republican party—are able to place themselves on the liberalism-conservatism dimension. The ability of respondents to conceive of their position on liberalism-conservatism relative to their own party is greater among strong Republicans than among strong Democrats.

Let us now turn briefly to a discussion of those respondents who define their ideological position with regard to only one party, although they are few in number. The distribution of their positions is presented in Table 2-5. Interestingly, as these data show, such individuals are more likely to define their own position relative to their own party than they are to define it relative to the opposition party, but the differences are not great.

The distribution of Democratic identifiers vis-à-vis the Democratic party is relatively flat, with some tendency toward liberalism, thus exerting a potential pull to the left on the party. This pull is also reflected in the liberalism of Democrats who classified themselves only with regard to the Republican party.

Among Republican identifiers the distribution relative to that party is even flatter, although again some tendency toward liberalism is manifested. Most Republicans who classify themselves only with regard to the Democratic party see themselves as more conservative than that party. Independents who classify themselves with regard to only one party seem to fall toward the middle of the spectrum, i.e., more conservative than the Democratic party or more liberal than the Republican party. The Independents in this group seem to exert a moderating influence.

The relationship for the respondents between party identification and

**Table 2-5**

**Liberalism-Conservatism of Respondents Who Defined Their Political Positions Relative to Only One Political Party (N=124)**

| | Political Position | | |
| --- | --- | --- | --- |
| | Democrat (N=70) (Percent) | Republican (N=27) (Percent) | Independent (N-27) (Percent) |
| More liberal than Democratic party | 20 | 7 | 19 |
| Same as Democratic party | 17 | – | 4 |
| More conservative than Democratic party | 16 | 33 | 33 |
| More liberal than Republican party | 30 | 22 | 22 |
| Same as Republican party | 1 | 19 | 7 |
| More conservative than Republican party | 16 | 19 | 15 |
| Total | 100 | 100 | 100 |

liberalism-conservatism in regard to *both parties* is presented in Table 2-6. Again, this table deals only with those respondents who rated themselves relative to both parties on the liberalism-conservatism dimension and agreed that the Republican party was more conservative than the Democratic party. These data suggest that strong partisans tend to be more extreme in their political views than are the parties they support, i.e., strong Democrats tend to be more liberal than the Democratic party and strong Republicans tend to be more conservative than the Republican party.

As a group, Republican identifiers are more likely than Democratic identifiers to place themselves relative to the major parties. Moreover, strength of partisanship is related to the presence of ideology among Republicans but not among Democrats. That is, strong Republicans (52%) are considerably more likely than weak Republicans (33%) to be ideologues, whereas there is no apparent difference in this regard between strong and weak Democratic identifiers (21% of each group). This evidence indicates that strength of affiliation is in this sense more consequential for Republicans than for Democrats.

Returning to Table 2-6, weak partisans are less likely to see their political positions as similar to that of the parties they choose. Rather, they are either more liberal or more conservative than their party. In the aggregate, the leanings of weak partisans are in a conservative direction. Weak Democrats are more likely to place themselves in the middle of the spectrum, and slightly more likely to say they are more conservative than both parties than they are to answer that they are more liberal than both parties. Weak Republicans are about equally likely to see themselves as more conservative than both parties and as occupying middle-of-the-road positions.

Independents who express partisan leanings tend to be conservative. Those

**Table 2-6**
**Political Party Identification by Liberalism-Conservatism (N=175)**

|  | Strong Dem. (N=22) (Percent) | Weak Dem. (N=37) (Percent) | Ind. Dem. (N=25) (Percent) | Ind. (N=20) (Percent) | Ind. Rep. (N=15) (Percent) | Weak Rep. (N=30) (Percent) | Strong Rep. (N=26) (Percent |
|---|---|---|---|---|---|---|---|
| Liberal | 36 | 22 | 16 | 50 | 13 | 17 | 8 |
| Democrat | 32 | 3 | – | 5 | 7 | – | – |
| Middle | 18 | 43 | 44 | 15 | 27 | 37 | 19 |
| Republican | 5 | 3 | 4 | – | 20 | 7 | 27 |
| Conservative | 9 | 30 | 36 | 30 | 33 | 40 | 46 |
| Total | 100 | 101 | 100 | 100 | 100 | 101 | 100 |

Note: Data on partisanship and strength or leaning are missing for two respondents who use the ideological labels.

who lean toward the Democratic party tend to do so from a middle-of-the-road position, and more than a third see themselves as more conservative than both parties. Those who lean toward the Republican party are more likely to do so from the conservative than from the middle-of-the-road position. Finally, Independents who state no preference tend to place themselves at the extremes, i.e., more liberal or more conservative than both parties. Independents with no leaning by no means appear to be strict middle-of-the-roaders.

In Table 2-7 position on the liberalism-conservatism dimension is related to party and strength of affiliation. As expected, a plurality of conservatives are Republicans. Similarly, as expected, the Republicans account for the fewest liberals but for most of the organizational Republican subgroup. Even more pronounced is the tendency of Democrats to account for the organizational Democrats. In reference to strength of affiliation, organizational partisans not surprisingly tend to be strong partisans. The other positions are favored by weak partisans. To hold an ideological position different from that of the party which one identifies with may involve breaking away from strong identification with the party.

### The Distribution of Political Affect

Our results are somewhat at variance with the most commonly used conceptualization of political partisanship in America. Questions regarding party identification and strength of partisanship or leaning in the case of Independents are most typically combined to produce the one-digit index of party choice depicted in Figure 2-1. The hypothetical distribution of this index reflects both the Democratic plurality in the American electorate, and the relatively small proportion of Americans who generally regard themselves as politically independent. While few researchers assume that this index represents an interval

**Table 2-7**
**Ideological Position by Party and Strength of Affiliation**

|  | Party (N=177) (Percent) | | | | Strength (N=116) (Percent) | | |
|  | Rep. | Dem. | Ind. | Total | S | W | Total |
|---|---|---|---|---|---|---|---|
| Liberal | 17 | 39 | 44 | 100 | 41 | 59 | 100 |
| Democrat | – | 80 | 20 | 100 | 88 | 12 | 100 |
| Middle-of-the-roader | 30 | 37 | 33 | 100 | 25 | 75 | 100 |
| Republican | 60 | 13 | 27 | 100 | 73 | 27 | 100 |
| Conservative | 42 | 18 | 30 | 100 | 37 | 63 | 100 |

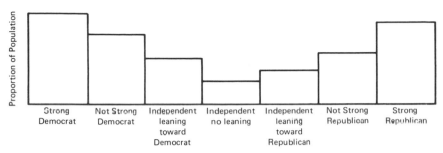

**Figure 2-1.** Hypothetical Distribution of a Population by the Index of Political Partisanship.

scale, the quality of ordinality has frequently been attributed to it. Thus party choice is conceived of as a dimension *bounded at the poles* by the strong partisan positions.[2] The strong partisan positions therefore are frequently represented as the most extreme positions. Strength of partisanship in this view may be seen to increase from the central positions of the Independents toward the extremes of the strong partisans.

Our findings on the other hand indicate that the distribution of political affect is much broader than the conceptualization presented in Figure 2-1, and that the strong partisan positions do not define the poles of this distribution. Rather, there are Independents *beyond* these polar positions who, rather than being "floating voters" might be either excluded from the political system or serve as the bases of support of extremist or third-party movements. In addition there are Independents with partisan leanings, and there are weak and strong partisans, who occupy political positions beyond the perceived positions of the parties they support. We will more fully consider the distribution of the electorate by referring back to Table 2-6.

The data presented in Table 2-6 serve as the source of the distribution of the Detroit electorate presented in Figure 2-2. You will recall that respondents were included in Table 2-6 under the constraint that they placed the Republican Party in a more conservative position than they placed the Democratic Party. The entries in Figure 2-2 assume an additional rational constraint: that people choose the political party whose position is compatible with their own ideological position. Thus, entries in Figure 2-2 represent only those cells within the dark lines of Table 2-6 giving us a new N of 140.[3] These people may be regarded as ideologues in the sense that they hold a position on the liberalism-conservatism dimension that seems to determine their party choice (cf. Shapiro, 1969). Partisans or Independents of partisan leaning who hold positions similar to or more extreme than the opposing party are excluded (N=35).

The data in Figure 2-2 will be used later to draw inferences regarding the

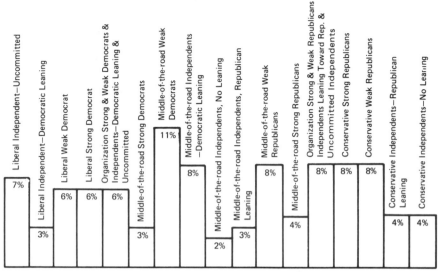

**Figure 2-2.** Liberalism-Conservatism and Strength of Party Support.

appropriate strategies for political parties to optimize their position among the electorate. In addition, those Independents remaining after the imposition of the additional constraint will be considered in a separate section. We hope that such an analysis will afford us greater insight into the range of distribution of political affect.

We have seen how ideologues are almost equally as likely to be Republicans, Democrats, or Independents. This finding indicates that, relative to the more numerous Democrats, there is a considerably greater ability among the Republicans and Independents to recognize ideological labels. Moreover, when considering those who do put ideological labels to use, we encountered a more general tendency toward *uniformity* (Table 2-2) and *ideological consistency* (Tables 2-2 and 2-6) among Republicans in comparison with the Democrats.

By *uniformity* we simply mean that there is a greater consensus among the Republicans regarding where they place themselves on the liberalism-conservatism dimension. By *ideological consistency* we are referring both to the ability to place onself in a logical position and to the selection of the political party most compatible with one's position on the liberalism-conservatism dimension. With this and the previous chapter defining the composition of the subgroups central to our analysis, we are prepared for the investigation of differences among these subgroups.

# 3 Ideologues vs. Nonideologues: How Different?

## Introduction

This part of our investigation concerns the ability to place oneself in relation to the liberalism-conservatism of the major parties. Five separate groups are defined by the recognition of ideological labels. Table 3-1 shows the distribution of the sample by use of ideological labels.

One limitation in any comparison is that the number of inconsistents and one party labelers is small relative to the ideologue and nonideologue categories. With only a few exceptions across the attitude measures, both one-party labeler groups show similar responses, and fall close to the nonideologues in their responses. We may surmise that while one-party labelers express partial recognition of the terms "liberal" or "conservative," they do not understand these terms as indicated by the inability to match these terms with both parties. More likely, one-party labelers are nonideologues who vaguely recognize the terms, but have little or no understanding of them. The indistinctiveness of their response patterns relative to nonideologues supports this conclusion. The other small group, the inconsistents, show a recognition of the terms liberal and conservative, but their answers do not reveal knowledge of the popular image of the major parties. On a clear majority of attitude items, inconsistents are the most conservative group. Our comparisons will deal mainly with the larger ideologue and nonideologue groups.

## Ideology and Social Background

We now move on to an examination of the social backgrounds of ideologues. Social factors tell us a considerable amount about differences within the

**Table 3-1**
**Recognition of Ideological Labels (N=640)**

| Label | Percent | (N) |
|---|---|---|
| Ideologue | 28 | (177) |
| Inconsistent ideologue | 3 | ( 20) |
| Democratic labelers | 10 | ( 61) |
| Republican labelers | 10 | ( 65) |
| Nonideologue | 49 | (317) |

electorate. As Milbrath (1965:110) notes, "The greatest quantity of research on political participation has related that behavior to social position variables." The distinct pattern of the ideologues can first of all be traced back to the urban-rural factor. Just over half the total number of respondents (N=323) were born and raised outside the Detroit area. Since "persons living in urbanized environments encounter more stimuli about politics than those living in the country" (Milbrath, 1965:45) we might expect that ideologues are more likely to come from large cities than the nonideologues. This is in fact the case. Some 41 percent of the ideologues were born and raised in a large city, whereas only 28 percent of the nonideologues fall into the same category (see Table 3-2).

Our ideologues come from consistently higher social strata than do our nonideologues. Table 3-2 presents the relationship between ideology and selected background factors. The ideologues have the highest occupational status when compared with the rest of the sample. Forty-two percent of them are in managerial, professional, and technical occupations, as against 30 percent for the sample as a whole.

It is almost a truism that persons of high education are more likely to have greater knowledge of and more sophistication about politics (Milbrath, 1965:68). Those who lack secondary or higher education tend to shut out political stimuli and as Milbrath says, "Exposure to stimuli about politics increases the quantity and sharpness of political knowledge, stimulates interest, contributes to the decisiveness of political choices, and firms up attachment to a party or candidate" (Milbrath, 1965:39-40). Not surprisingly then, we find some 48 percent of the ideologues, as against 29 percent of the total sample and only 17 percent of the nonideologues have had at least some college education. Moreover, this educational advantage has persisted through at least two generations. Twenty percent of the ideologues report that their fathers had some college education, as against 12 percent for the sample as a whole, and only 8 percent for nonideologues.

Similarly, there are sharp income differences between ideologues and nonideologues.[1] Interestingly, this variable does not discriminate as well as occupation and education between ideologues, inconsistent ideologues, and Republican labelers. Roughly one-fourth of each of these groups reported annual incomes of $17,000 or more, as against 7 percent for nonideologues.

Sex also sharply distinguishes the groups. Fully 64 percent of ideologues are males, while only 37 percent of nonideologues are males. Given that men move more in environments having more political stimuli than women, and so are more likely than women to be psychologically involved in politics (Berelson et al., 1954; Lazarsfeld et al., 1944; Almond and Verba, 1963), this is the pattern one would expect. Nonideologues also are the least likely to be homeowners. This small difference is not surprising since homeowners are somewhat more likely to be politically active than renters (Milbrath, 1965:133). Religious differences in recognition of ideological labels are slight.

27

**Table 3-2**
**Ideology by Selected Background Factors**

| Use of Ideological Label | Occupation — Percent Professional, Technical and Managerial | Education — Percent Some College+ | Father's Education — Percent Some College+ | Family Income — Percent $17,000+ | Sex — Percent Male | Home Ownership — Percent Rent | Religion Prot. | Religion Percent Cath. | Religion Jew | Type of Community Raised in as Child — Percent Large City |
|---|---|---|---|---|---|---|---|---|---|---|
| Ideologue (177) | 42 | 48 | 20 | 25 | 64 | 15 | 49 | 40 | 2 | 41 |
| Inconsistent (20) | 21 | 30 | 10 | 25 | 45 | 15 | 40 | 55 | 5 | 33 |
| Republican (61) | 31 | 36 | 13 | 23 | 41 | 15 | 49 | 46 | 2 | 26 |
| Democrat (65) | 23 | 29 | 11 | 9 | 57 | 12 | 40 | 52 | 3 | 21 |
| Nonideologue (317) | 25 | 17 | 8 | 7 | 37 | 20 | 51 | 42 | 1 | 28 |
| Total (640) | 30 | 29 | 12 | 14 | 48 | 17 | 49 | 43 | 2 | 31 |

Note: The N for type of community raised in as a child is only 323.

### Ideology and Issue Orientations

*Views on Social Welfare and*
*Civil Liberties*

Here we will consider the attitudes of ideologues and nonideologues. We certainly are not suggesting that we are tapping all the distinctive issue arenas which the liberalism-conservatism dimension represents, but we do have a fairly broad set of questions on domestic affairs.

With regard to social welfare, ideologues are found consistently to be the most conservative group. Respondents were asked, "Do you think the federal government should in some way provide jobs for people who are unemployed and can't find work?" A large minority of ideologues (43 percent) give unqualified approval to the use of government power in the area of employment. Among nonideologues a small majority (52 percent) favors such governmental action (p < .10).[2]

Similar but also statistically insignificant results were obtained on the issue of federal support of poorer schools.[3] The question asked, "Some neighborhoods have schools with rundown buildings and less-trained teachers than other neighborhoods. Do you think the federal government should provide more money to bring the poor schools up to the standard of the better schools, or that the government shouldn't do this?" Ideologues (42 percent in favor) again tend to be in opposition while nonideologues (57 percent) are somewhat more likely to give an answer favorable to government intervention.

On another matter of governmental intervention respondents were asked, "Do you think the federal government should guarantee free medical and hospital care for everyone?" The result is not quite significant, yet a similar pattern is seen to hold, ideologues being less likely to answer in the positive. Overall, while the differences are not sharp, the trend of the results does indicate a somewhat greater tendency toward conservatism on social welfare issues among ideologues.

On the other hand, in the civil liberties area, ideologues have distinctive attitudes indicating a consistently liberal position. Almost two-thirds (64 percent) of ideologues feel that police should be allowed to wiretap telephone conversations if it is necessary to solve crimes. Yet fully four-fifths (81 percent) of nonideologues express a belief that the police should be able to do so. Even though a basic law and order orientation seems dominant throughout the electorate—the majority of the sample (75 percent) being in favor of allowing police to wiretap telephones—those persons who are ideologues are significantly less likely to condone the use of wiretapping.

The results on the wiretapping issue are mirrored in the other measures of attitudes on civil liberties issues. Approximately one-third (36 percent) of ideologues think that censorship of movies is acceptable. This compares to a majority (52 percent) of nonideologues who feel certain movies with nude actors should be banned. Finally, when asked about the danger posed by Communists, ideologues (21 percent) are somewhat more likely than nonideologues (12 percent) to believe that Communists are no danger. While this last item is not quite statistically significant, these results do confirm the apparent tendency of ideologues to be more liberal than nonideologues on matters relating to civil liberties.

*Civil Rights Views*

A large part of the 1969 Detroit Area Study survey was devoted to civil rights matters. In regard to civil rights issues, a number of significant differences are apparent. There are three questions designed to reveal respondent beliefs about the existence of the social and economic disadvantages faced by blacks. These measures concern unemployment among blacks, the relative quality of white and black housing, and the quality of teachers in black areas. On each item ideologues are significantly more likely to express awareness of the plight of blacks (Table 3-3).

Certainly one of the most striking aspects of this table is the consistency of differences between the ideologue and nonideologue groups.

We find that respondents who are ideologues (42 percent) are twice as likely as nonideologues (21 percent) to acknowledge that the quality of teachers is worse in black areas of Detroit. Similarly, only one-third of the nonideologues feel that unemployment is greater among black residents of Detroit. A majority (53 percent) of ideologues see the unemployment rate of blacks as a lot greater. A somewhat sharper difference is apparent on the question of housing quality. Ideologues are nearly twice as likely to express a belief that black housing is a lot worse.

In Table 3-3 the results of questions related to acknowledgement of racial discrimination are also presented. Respondents were asked: "Would you say there's a lot of discrimination against blacks when they look for a job in the Detroit area or little discrimination?" and "Would you say there's a lot of discrimination against blacks trying to get a home or little discrimination?" In the area of housing, 61 percent of ideologues, as compared to a minority of nonideologues (48 percent) believe that there is a lot of discrimination against blacks. Even though the overall perception of job discrimination is much lower than the similar awareness in the area of housing, ideologues tend to be distinct here too. They are twice as likely as nonideologues to perceive discrimination against blacks in jobs. The difference on the question of job discrimination is statistically significant, and the housing item is nearly significant ($p < .10$). It is evident from their answers that ideologues tend toward a stronger appreciation of racial discrimination than do nonideologues.

**Table 3-3**
**Ideology and Perception of Blacks in American Society**

| Ideology | Perception of Black Disadvantages Area of Black Disadvantage | | | | | | Perception of Racial Discrimination Area of Discrimination | |
| | Quality of Black Housing | | Quality of Teachers in Black Schools | | Unemployment among Blacks | | Discrimination in Employment | Discrimination in Housing |
| | Lot Worse (Percent) | Not Much Difference (Percent) | Same (Percent) | Black Worse (Percent) | Lot Greater | Black Same as among Whites (Percent) | Percent a lot | Percent a lot |
|---|---|---|---|---|---|---|---|---|
| Ideologues | 57 | 24 | 56 | 42 | 53 | 21 | 20 | 61 |
| Nonideologues | 31 | 43 | 77 | 21 | 33 | 40 | 10 | 48 |

Note: Percentagizing is done by rows. Percents do not add to 100 because not all categories are presented. For ideologues the base N ranges from 171-175, and for nonideologues from 276-306 due to missing data.

We might expect that perceptions of the social and economic disadvantages of blacks and racial discrimination be associated with beliefs about the reasons for these situations. To ascertain the reasons respondents thought blacks to be disadvantaged respondents were asked: "Where blacks are behind whites in such things as jobs or income or housing, do you think this is mainly due to something about blacks themselves, or mainly due to the way whites have treated blacks in the past?" This question perhaps more accurately asks, "Where does the responsibility for the inferior position of blacks lie, in some inadequacy of blacks or in racial discrimination?" Some three-fifths (61 percent) of the nonideologue group are prone to feel that blacks are behind in jobs or housing due to something about themselves. Ideologues (44 percent) are significantly less likely to place the blame of black disadvantages on some inadequacy of their own.

Respondents were asked about their fear of violence by blacks: "How much danger, if any, do you think there is of groups of blacks from the inner city going out to white areas and suburbs to commit violence on whites?" The results on this question are presented in Table 3-4. Approximately one out of six ideologues (15 percent) believe it very probable that blacks will commit violence on suburban whites, while nearly one-quarter (24 percent) of nonideologues see this violence as a distinct probability. Although this is not a sharp difference, there is apparently a greater tendency for nonideologues to feel threatened by blacks. To further demonstrate this tendency the results from an index of perceived fear of blacks is presented in Table 3-5.[4] The greater tendency of nonideologues to believe in blacks being a threat to whites is readily seen.

Next we attempted to examine the possible link between perceived threat from blacks and liberalism or conservatism on civil disorders. Respondents were asked: "What do you think is the most important thing the city government in Detroit could do to keep a riot like the one in 1967 from breaking out again?" We collapsed the responses into categories which stress improving conditions and those which emphasize repression.[5] That fear of blacks is translated into a tendency toward repression is evident. Ideologues (30 percent) are nearly twice as likely as nonideologues (16 percent) to express a belief in the need to treat,

**Table 3-4**
**Ideology and Perceived Danger of Black Violence (N=487)**

| Ideology | Great | Some | Little or None | Total |
|---|---|---|---|---|
| | | (Percent) | | |
| Ideologue (177) | 15 | 40 | 45 | 100 |
| Nonideologue (310) | 24 | 42 | 34 | 100 |

**Table 3-5**
**Ideology and the Index of Perceived Fear of Blacks (N=492)**

| Ideology | Low | | | | | | High | Total |
|---|---|---|---|---|---|---|---|---|
| | 1 | 2 | 3 | 4 | 5 | 6 | 7 | |
| Ideologue (176) | 6 | 21 | 22 | 30 | 17 | 2 | 1 | 100 |
| Nonideologue (316) | 2 | 10 | 29 | 25 | 22 | 9 | 3 | 100 |

by one means or another, the causes of racial disorders. We might conclude that this statistically significant difference indicates a greater liberalism on their part.

A related item inquiring whether respondents believe that it is a good idea for whites to organize against violence by blacks shows ideologues to be somewhat more, but not significantly, against such action. This "vigilante" item might well be considered among the civil liberties questions.

Concerning social distance items, ideologues are found to express more positive feelings than nonideologues about contacts with blacks. However consistent, the magnitudes of these differences do not reach significance. The measures of interracial social distance include a series of three questions referring to contact at a party, and in dating and marriage situations. On this party-date-marry series of questions, the largest difference between ideologues and nonideologues is 10 percent. An additional item asks respondents if a white mother should allow her daughter to play with a black child at home, at school, or never to play with black children. These results also indicate the slightly greater willingness of ideologues (84 percent) to allow the black child to play at the white home. This compares to 74 percent among the nonideologues.

An index of social distance constructed from the above four items shows the differences between ideologues and nonideologues most readily.[6] In Table 3-6 we present the results on this index.

**Table 3-6**
**Ideology and the Index of Social Distance (N=470)**

| Ideology | Social Distance (Percent) | | | Total |
|---|---|---|---|---|
| | Low (1-3) | Medium (4-6) | High (7-9) | |
| Ideologue (173) | 31 | 45 | 24 | 100 |
| Nonideologue (297) | 29 | 37 | 34 | 100 |

Finally, respondents were asked whether they ever got together with blacks, apart from neighbors, in any social or recreational activities. While 27 percent of ideologues get together socially with blacks, this drops to 20 percent for nonideologues. In spite of the significantly greater tendency among ideologues to acknowledge the prevalence of black disadvantages and the existence of racial discrimination, they are not found to express a significantly greater positive affect toward interracial contact. This finding perhaps accounts in part for the results on a series of three fair hiring questions. Ideologues are only slightly more likely than nonideologues to express positive feelings regarding the hiring of a black.

There are also several questions regarding aspects of residential integration. Attitudes concerning residential integration should be indirect measures of interracial social distance. These items ascertained whether a respondent would sell his house to a black: if he thought neighbors would be willing to sell, if he would sell to a respected Negro doctor, if he would change his opinion under the urging of his neighbors, and what respondents thought about the open housing issue, etc.

On the question of whether a respondent would be willing to sell his house to a black, ideologues are no more likely to express a willingness to sell than are nonideologues. The distributions of both groups on this question are nearly identical. Following up this question is a series of items which were designed to reveal more specifically attitudes on the housing question. Slight differences are found on occasion. For example, on the question of a community-wide vote on the open housing issue, some 78 percent of ideologues feel a home owner should decide for himself, while 83 percent of nonideologues favor owners' rights over open housing regulations. However, we do not find significant differences in a single item on this series of questions.

This similarity between ideologues and nonideologues also holds on the issue of bussing black children from an overcrowded school to a school where a child of the respondent is attending. There is one question relating to residential attitudes on which ideologues are distinct from nonideologues. This question asks respondents whether they believe blacks prefer residential integration to segregation. Some 46 percent of ideologues feel that blacks prefer residential integration, whereas nonideologues (32 percent) are less likely to see blacks as desiring racially mixed neighborhoods.

If this last question reveals the respondent's *own* preferences regarding the desirability of segregated versus integrated housing, we might conclude that ideologues are more favorable on residential integration. Perhaps this question is simply another measure of awareness. Although ideologues appear to be more aware of the existence of racial discrimination, they are not significantly more likely than nonideologues to hold positive views concerning interracial contact.

In sum, ideologues express somewhat less favorable views on social welfare issues, yet tend toward more favorable views on civil liberties, feel less threatened by black Americans, and are evidently more ready to acknowledge the existence of racial discrimination relative to nonideologues. These results hold independently of the direction of ideological leaning among ideologues. Our findings can be considered in the context of Lipset's (1968) views on liberalism and conservatism. Lipset suggests the existence of two liberalism-conservatism dimensions, one involving *economic* and the other *noneconomic* attitudes. These dimensions do not necessarily correlate positively, and Lipset indicates that the poor are liberal on the former but not the latter, while the well-to-do are liberal on the latter but not the former. Given the knowledge that our ideologues come from *higher* social strata than do our nonideologues, we find a pattern of ideologues being *conservative* on social welfare (economic) but *liberal* on civil rights (noneconomic) views, to be quite consistent with Lipset's formulation.

However, it is most noteworthy that many of these differences in attitudes between ideologues and nonideologues are *smaller* than we might have anticipated on the basis of the social status differences, particularly with regard to occupation and education. Indeed, had we sufficient cases to reliably sustain multivariate analysis, we would expect that *partialling* out the effects of socioeconomic status might well remove the attitudinal differences between ideologues and nonideologues.

**Ideology and Political Sophistication**

Not surprisingly, ideologues are found to be distinctive on measures of political sophistication. In Table 3-7 the results of a question on mention of national leaders are presented. Respondents were asked to name two national figures they admire. We assume that mention of leaders admired is chiefly a function of the number of national leaders known. Since we know that not all Americans even know the name of the President, there could easily be some differences among levels of the electorate on this question. While nearly three out of four ideologues (71 percent) mention two leaders they admire, less than half (45 percent) of nonideologues give the names of two leaders.

**Table 3-7**
**Ideology and Mention of National Leaders (N=494)**

| Ideology | Number of Leaders Mentioned (Percent) | | | |
|---|---|---|---|---|
| | None | One | Two | Total |
| Ideologue (177) | 10 | 19 | 71 | 100 |
| Nonideologue (317) | 27 | 28 | 45 | 100 |

We felt that it might be instructive to ask if there are any differences in the leaders mentioned by ideologues and nonideologues. Respondents were asked to mention only living national figures. We felt that respondents who were nonideologues would perhaps be more likely to mention dead leaders or local figures. However, these differences were insignificant; some 4 percent of ideologues mentioned dead or local leaders as compared to 9 percent amont the nonideologue group. It appears that those nonideologues who do mention a national figure are nearly as likely as ideologues to select an appropriate person.

As the measure of general sophistication, we used "don't know" responses. The manner in which we approached the question of sophistication was to calculate the proportion of "don't know" responses separately for each of 70 attitude items. These items included all social welfare, civil liberties, and civil rights questions, as well as the considerable number of agree-disagree items. Then the average percentage of "don't know" responses was calculated.

While ideologues make up 28 percent of the entire sample, they account for an average of only 7 percent of the total "don't know" responses. Nonideologues, however, who constitute 49 percent of the sample account for 74 percent of the "don't know" responses. We can readily see that ideologues are underrepresented, while nonideologues are overrepresented, in "don't know" responses from Table 3-8. Here we present select items from each area so as to contrast the "don't know" response of ideologues and nonideologues. Although the size of the "don't know" category varies from item to item, a very clear pattern emerges demonstrating that ideologues are apparently more sophisticated in their responses.

### Ideology and Personality Characteristics

We have recently passed the twentieth anniversary of the publication of *The Authoritarian Personality*.[7] Following the tradition of this book, a considerable body of literature has developed. Lane (1962:415) speaks of this approach to the study of ideological development as one that "hardly employs the concept of ideology at all; rather in a voluminous literature, it attacks attitudes and beliefs piecemeal." The many contributions to the causes and conditions of social beliefs need to be pulled together.

Milbrath (1965:84) believes that "Despite the rash of studies, there is relatively little evidence in the form of substantiated propositions about the impact of authoritarianism on political behavior." Rokeach (1960) and many experimenters have traced the inadequacy of the approach of Adorno et al. (1950), in part to the problem of response set bias. Instruments should allow for the expression of both an authoritarian left and right. There is some question of the validity of the measure of authoritarianism since the response set problem is obvious, "but it is certainly not clear that all of the personality dynamics implied by the 'authoritarianism syndrome' are documented by the response set

**Table 3-8**
**Percentages of "Don't Know" Responses on Select Attitude Items by Ideology**

| Don't Know Responses on Select Items | Ideology | | Total N of Don't Knows |
|---|---|---|---|
| | Nonideologue | Ideologue | |
| | (Percent) | | |
| Social welfare | | | |
| federal provision | | | |
| of jobs | 80 | 0 | 5 |
| Free medical care | 100 | 0 | 5 |
| Civil liberties | | | |
| U.S. Communists are a danger | 80 | 0 | 15 |
| Whites should organize against blacks | 64 | 27 | 11 |
| Agree-Disagree items | | | |
| To compromise with enemies is dangerous | 68 | 13 | 31 |
| We cannot understand mental patients | 73 | 20 | 15 |
| Boys who wear long hair not allowed in school | 90 | 10 | 10 |
| Perception of black disadvantages | | | |
| Quality of black housing | 72 | 9 | 11 |
| Quality of teachers in black schools | 67 | 10 | 58 |
| Reason for blacks being behind | 67 | 7 | 15 |
| Black violence | | | |
| Danger of blacks going to white areas to commit violence | 88 | 0 | 8 |
| Prevention of racial disturbance | 75 | 12 | 51 |
| Stereotyping | | | |
| Blacks are content | 83 | 4 | 24 |
| Blacks and sports | 100 | 0 | 4 |
| Blacks and morals | 89 | 0 | 18 |
| Social distance | | | |
| White child play with black child | 91 | 0 | 11 |
| Black marry relative of respondent | 67 | 0 | 6 |
| Housing | | | |
| Sell to black couple | 64 | 18 | 11 |
| Sell to black doctor | 87 | 13 | 15 |
| Support open housing regulation | 100 | 0 | 3 |

Note: Rows do not in all cases add to 100 percent because the inconsistent and one-party labeler categories are not presented.

alone" (Campbell et al., 1960:511). Rokeach finds dogmatism scores to be related to a negligible degree with scores on liberalism-conservatism tests. Thus he concludes that the dogmatism scale is actually measuring *general* authoritarianism, since it is evident along all positions of the political spectrum (Rokeach, 1960:121-122). However, "bigotry has a somewhat greater affinity with right-of-center ideologies by its very nature" (Rokeach, 1960:123).

As a result of such difficulties, few results in the area of personality and politics are conclusive. It is not even known if authoritarians are more likely to be Democrats or Republicans, liberals or conservatives (Milbrath, 1961:85). Campbell et al. (1960) acknowledge that some efforts have been devoted to showing that some personality types are differentially attracted to one party or the other. While they expect little from the association between deeper personality factors and partisan choice, they admit that personality and reactions to policy questions may show considerable interaction. Issues "tend to pose alternatives that gear into personality dynamics in a much clearer way than is true of partisan choice. . . ." For example, the "authoritarians should be less sympathetic with the civil rights of minority groups and should resist the notion that the federal government might be concerned with their welfare" (Campbell et al., 1960:511).

All the proposed personality dimensions—authoritarianism, dogmatism, misanthropy, etc.—although they have never been systematically treated within one research effort, tap a syndrome of *externalization*,[8] that is, a tendency to project inner conflicts usually involving antisocial impulses onto the outer world. The scales such as the F scale developed to measure various aspects of this syndrome describe certain structural characteristics of the attitudes of the externalizing personality. The list of previously demonstrated characteristics is long, including rigidity, status orientation, conformity, alienation, powerlessness, stereotyping, hostility, social distance, and so on.

We will now investigate, in a limited manner, the relationships between ideology and personality characteristics. Small differences are apparent, and it is the ideologues who reveal the *most positive* characteristics.[9]

An index of *fascism* is constructed on four agree-disagree items (see Table 3-9). Ideologues tend to rank lower on this measure (43 percent agreeing to all four questions), whereas nonideologues tend to rank higher, a majority of 60 percent agreeing to all fascism items. The finding that a large percentage of the total sample ranks high on this index perhaps confirms the basic law and order orientation of the electorate.

The next items we will consider are thought to measure *dogmatism*. Some 29 percent of the ideologues rank high on the index of dogmatism, while 34 percent of the nonideologues appear dogmatic. The underlying desire for structure by a dogmatic mind might be of some assistance in accounting for our finding that nonideologues appear to be slightly more closed minded. On the other hand, we must note the relatively minimal difference between ideologues and nonideologues, although this difference is in the expected direction. With regard to *misanthropy* ideologues are shown to be the most trusting group.

**Table 3-9**
**Ideology and Indices of Personality Measures**

| Ideology | Percent Agreeing with All Items | | | |
|---|---|---|---|---|
| | Fascism | Dogmatism | Misanthropy | Status Concern |
| | | | (Percent) | |
| Ideologue | 43 | 29 | 11 | 9 |
| Nonideologue | 60 | 34 | 22 | 16 |

Personality measures index:

*Fascism items:*

1. Obedience and respect for authority are the most important virtues children should learn.
2. Young people sometimes get rebellious ideas, but as they grow up they ought to get over them and settle down.
3. No decent, normal person would think of hurting a close friend or relative.
4. Most of our social problems could be solved if we could somehow get rid of the immoral and crooked people.

*Dogmatism items:*

1. To compromise with one's enemies is dangerous because it usually leads to betrayal of one's own side.
2. There are two kinds of people in the world, those who are for truth and those who are against truth.

*Misanthropy items:*

1. Most people can be trusted.
2. Most people will take advantage of another person if given a chance.

*Status concern items:*

1. The raising of one's social position is one of the most important goals in life.
2. One should always try to live in a highly respectable community even if it means sacrificing other things.

Note: Percentaging is done by rows. The number of cases varies on these indices due to differences in missing data. For ideologues the Ns range from 172-177, and for nonideologues the range is from 300-316.

Finally, we looked at the possibility that differences are revealed by an index of *status concern*. And in fact, ideologues are slightly less likely than nonideologues to express a concern for social status.

On the basis of these results perhaps a tentative picture of the association between the use of ideological labels and personality emerges. Nonideologues appear to be somewhat more authoritarian, more dogmatic, and less trusting than ideologues. What these differences in personality characteristics would lead us to believe is that ideologues, as we have defined them, are less likely to be closed minded. However, these differences are not statistically significant except for the fascism index.

We went on to examine the distribution of ideologues and nonideologues on a series of stereotyping items. Again, while ideologues are less likely to accept character traits as typical of black Americans, the apparent differences are not significant.

Summing up, in comparing ideologues with the rest of the sample, we found the former to be of consistently higher socioeconomic status. On the bases of a fairly wide range of attitude measures several differences among respondents, based on their ability to recognize ideological labels, were apparent. In addition, the question of the relationship between ideology and personality characteristics was raised.

Although in this last section it seems that there are few if any differences worth reporting, the direction of the results is consistent with the greater awareness of ideologues as indicated by their socioeconomic background, political sophistication, and perception of black disadvantages and social discrimination. Yet, with the exception of apparent differences in their level of awareness, ideologues are perhaps less distinct than we might expect.

# 4 Liberals vs. Conservatives: Correlates of Ideological Position

## Introduction

We have suggested in the previous chapter areas in which political ideologues are distinctive from nonideologues. Now we will concentrate on an internal analysis of the ideologues. The measures of liberalism-conservatism allow us to differentiate between positions along this dimension. In Figure 1-1 the distribution of respondents by ideological position was presented.

It is indeed interesting that so few respondents place themselves in the position of the major parties. However, the small Ns of these positions make comparisons across the liberalism-conservatism dimension less reliable than we would like. Yet we have described the voluntary nature of this category, so those respondents who locate their views close to the positions of the parties appear to do so out of a relatively strong commitment to these positions. In addition, we should consider the consistency which the response patterns of the organizational partisans reveal. Perhaps then some comparison with respondents in other positions is acceptable. However, the small Ns require that the organizational partisans be excluded from significance testing.

With regard to the distribution of ideologues in Figure 1-1 it is noteworthy that there are considerably fewer liberals (N=41) than conservatives (N=57). This is in spite of the fact that Democrats whom we might expect to fall on the left account for a near majority of the total sample.

## The Liberalism-Conservatism Dimension and Social Background

Several interesting findings emerge from an analysis of socioeconomic status within the ideologue subgroup (see Table 4-1). Respondents who placed themselves to the right of both parties, to the left of both parties, or in the middle-of-the-road tend to be of higher educational and occupational status than respondents who feel that their political position is the same as that of one of the two political parties. Among the three nonorganizational positions (liberal, middle-of-the-road, conservative) there is no gradation from left to right with regard to these social background factors. Rather, the relationships are curvilinear, peaking at the middle-of-the-road position. The middle-of-the-roaders, in turn, are more similar to the liberals than to the conservatives.

41

**Table 4-1**
**Liberalism-Conservatism by Selected Background Factors**

| Position | Occupation<br>Percent Professional, Technical and Managerial | Education<br>Percent Some College+ | Father's Education<br>Percent Some College+ | Family Income<br>Percent $17,000+ | Age<br>Percent 18-39 | 60+ | Sex<br>Percent Male | Home Ownership<br>Percent Rent | Religion<br>Prot. | Percent Cath. | Jew | Type of Community Raised in as Child<br>Percent Large City |
|---|---|---|---|---|---|---|---|---|---|---|---|---|
| Liberal (41) | 41 | 51 | 30 | 22 | 54 | 5 | 76 | 24 | 51 | 34 | 5 | 43 |
| Democrat (10) | 30 | 30 | 10 | 20 | 30 | 0 | 70 | 0 | 30 | 70 | 0 | 33 |
| Middle (54) | 51 | 54 | 22 | 22 | 44 | 7 | 61 | 18 | 46 | 48 | 0 | 44 |
| Republican (15) | 33 | 40 | 20 | 20 | 33 | 0 | 53 | 13 | 73 | 20 | 0 | 9 |
| Conservative (57) | 37 | 44 | 12 | 32 | 47 | 7 | 61 | 7 | 53 | 37 | 4 | 52 |
| Total (177) | 42 | 48 | 20 | 25 | 46 | 7 | 64 | 15 | 49 | 43 | 2 | 41 |

Note: The N for type of community raised in as child is only 86.

However, when considering father's education, the liberals show the greatest probability of coming from a higher status background, while in regard to family income, the conservatives tend to be of higher financial status than the rest of the ideologues. That no single group tends consistently toward higher status is also indicated by home ownership. Liberals are the most likely to rent rather than own their home, yet this may be explained in part by age differences. That liberals are more likely than any other group in the total sample to be male suggests that perhaps they are the most subject to political stimuli.

## The Liberalism-Conservatism Dimension
## and Issue Orientations

When we consider the attitude differences within the ideologue group, a general pattern of *increasing liberalism* from right to left is found. This pattern is complicated by those in the organizational positions who appear to be the most conservative groups.

It will be recalled that ideologues are apparently somewhat more conservative than nonideologues on social welfare matters. However, although ideologues and nonideologues show some small differences in the area of social welfare, there are no differences among ideologues. This suggests a uniformity in social welfare views among those members of the electorate who can place themselves relative to both parties.

Quite different results emerge when we consider civil liberties and civil rights items. Liberals tend to be more favorable in these areas than conservatives. Middle-of-the-roaders, true to their name, usually are found to fall between the liberal and conservative groups. It is evident, however, that the organizational partisans, whether closer to the Republican or Democratic party, are the most conservative group with regard to civil liberties and civil rights attitudes. The image of increasing liberalism right to left holds for most questions, except for the deviations of the organizational partisans.

The most frequently encountered pattern in order of descending liberalism of responses runs from liberals, middle-of-the-roaders, conservatives, to organizational Democrats and Republicans. Those respondents occupying organizational positions tend to be closer to the conservative group than to the middle or liberal categories. The similarity in the response patterns of those occupying organizational positions is not surprising if one considers that in 1968 voters favoring Humphrey and Nixon were much closer to one another in their attitudes than to those favoring Wallace (Wolfe, 1968). One might reasonably expect respondents who in 1969 placed themselves near to the parties of Humphrey and Nixon to be more alike in their attitudes than respondents who believe themselves to be more conservative than both major parties (presumably many of the Wallace voters would place themselves here).

In Table 4-2, results concerning the civil liberties issues are presented. On each of these questions relating to civil liberties liberals are less likely than conservatives to favor the abridgement of freedom in one form or another. And with the exception of the item on the danger posed by Communists, where they tie with liberals, middle-of-the-roaders do fall between the two ends of the dimension, generally closer to the conservatives. The sharpest difference between the two extreme groups is most apparent on the censorship item. Although this item is the only one where the differences are statistically significant, the others only approaching significance, these differences are quite consistent.

While only one-fifth (19 percent) of the liberals favor a ban on certain movies, nearly one-half the conservatives (48 percent) are likely to recommend such control. Similarly, while one in ten liberals thinks that it is a good idea for whites to organize so as to protect themselves against violence by blacks, fully one out of every four conservatives (26 percent) feels whites should get together to protect themselves. In 1968 an organization of suburban white housewives in Dearborn was formed in order to train these women in the use of firearms and in other defensive practices. This organization received a considerable amount of publicity, both local and national. We may suppose that memories from the summer of 1967 were vivid enough to prompt a significant minority of conservatives to favor such action.

Attitudes expressing perceived danger from another source also distinguish between liberals and conservatives. Some 39 percent of liberals see Communists as a great danger, whereas this increases to 55 percent among the conservatives. And finally, on the wiretapping issue, conservatives are somewhat (68 percent) more likely than liberals (52 percent) to favor such police procedure. Although organizational partisans are not always the most extreme in their answers (as on the censorship item), they are always found to be distinct from liberals.

**Table 4-2**
**Position on Liberalism-Conservatism Dimension and Civil Liberties Views**

| | | Civil Liberties Views | | |
| --- | --- | --- | --- | --- |
| Position | Police Wiretap Telephone— Percent Favor | Ban Movies with Nude Actors— Percent Favor Banning | Communist Danger— Percent Great Danger | Whites Organize against Blacks— Percent Good Idea |
| Liberal | 52 | 19 | 39 | 10 |
| Democrat | 80 | 40 | 70 | 33 |
| Middle-of-the-road | 61 | 36 | 39 | 20 |
| Republican | 80 | 47 | 53 | 40 |
| Conservative | 68 | 48 | 55 | 26 |

Note: Percentaging is done by rows. Due to differences in missing data, the total N ranges from 171-176.

A similar pattern is evident on civil rights issues. Due to the small Ns involved, we will not present in the following tables the responses of the organizational partisans. Without exception, however, organizational Democrats and Republicans are found to be closer to the conservatives than to the liberals, and most often they fall well beyond the conservatives in their responses.

Table 4-3 shows the results for liberals, middle-of-the-roaders, and conservatives on the perception of black disadvantages items. Each of these results is nearly, but not quite, significant. Liberals are the most likely to see the disadvantages faced by blacks in housing, education, and unemployment. While a majority of liberals feel that blacks are much worse off in each area, only a minority of the conservatives acknowledge such racial disadvantages. Middle-of-the-roaders fall in between, and on two of these items are closer to liberals than conservatives. A similar pattern is evident on measures of perception of racial discrimination in the areas of housing and employment. These differences, however, are not nearly significant.

Perhaps the most striking differences are evident on questions tapping the action component of racial attitudes. These results are either significant or nearly significant. Conservatives (28 percent) are four times as likely as liberals (7 percent) to have sold their home and moved away because blacks were moving into their neighborhood. The willingness to sell one's house to a black couple demonstrates how distinctive the liberals are in their racial attitudes. Some three-fifths of the liberals (61 percent) would sell their house to a black couple who could afford it. However, only about one-third of the conservatives (37 percent) are willing to sell to a black. Although middle-of-the-roaders are as unlikely to have moved away from a neighborhood because of incoming blacks as are liberals, they are no more willing to sell their home to a black than are the conservative group.

Of those who would sell their house to a black couple, a majority (64 percent) of the liberals would still sell their house even under pressure from worried neighbors, whereas some 50 percent of the middle group, and 35 percent of conservatives would go against the wishes of their neighbors. This result implies a greater tendency toward conformity among the less liberal. On the other hand, among those respondents who would not sell their house to a black couple, liberals (29 percent) are nearly twice as likely as conservatives (15 percent) to be willing to sell to a black who is a respected doctor.

Although we find a marked decline from the general disposition to sell one's house to the willingness to vote in favor of open housing, a difference between liberals and conservatives is still apparent. Liberals (24 percent) are much more likely than conservatives (7 percent) to support open housing in a community-wide vote. Middle-of-the-roaders appear to be the least consistent of the groups in these action situations. In their willingness to vote in favor of open housing, middle-of-the-roaders seem the most liberal; however, as mentioned before, they are no more likely to agree to sell their house to a black than are the conservatives.

**Table 4-3**
**Position on Liberalism-Conservatism Dimension, Perception of Black Disadvantages, and Action Items**

| | Area of Black Disadvantages | | | | | | | Action Items | | | | |
| | Quality of Black Housing | | | Quality of Teachers in Black Schools | | Unemployment among Blacks | | Moved Away from Black | Sell House to Black Couple | Still Sell House to Black under Pressure by Neighbors | Sell House to Black Doctor | Support Open Housing |
| Position | Little Worse | Lot Worse | Not Much Different | Same | Black Worse | Lot Greater among Black | Same as among Whites | Percent Yes | Percent Yes | Percent Yes | Percent Yes | Percent Yes |
|---|---|---|---|---|---|---|---|---|---|---|---|---|
| Liberal | 16 | 66 | 18 | 40 | 56 | 70 | 13 | 7 | 61 | 64 | 29 | 24 |
| Middle | 13 | 60 | 27 | 50 | 48 | 53 | 20 | 7 | 36 | 50 | 20 | 39 |
| Conservative | 28 | 47 | 25 | 67 | 33 | 41 | 26 | 28 | 37 | 35 | 15 | 7 |

Note: Percentaging is done by rows. Percents do not always add to 100 because not all categories are presented. There are a total of 152 liberals, middle-of-the-roaders, and conservatives, but due to differences in missing data the total N ranges from 147-152 on all except the contingency questions. On "neighborhood pressure" there are 54 responses, and on "sell to black Doctor" there are 77 responses.

Another question related to housing deals with the respondent's belief about the residential aspirations of blacks (N=140, due to missing data). Liberals (33 percent) are the least likely to feel that blacks want segregated residential areas, whereas identical majorities (56 percent) of the middle and conservative groups appear to believe that blacks prefer segregation. Similar tendencies are revealed by the question on support of bussing proposal (N=147, due to missing data). Liberals (63 percent) tend to support a proposal to bring black children to white schools, while some 47 percent of conservatives favor such action. Middle-of-the-roaders are nearly as likely as liberals (60 percent) to support a bussing proposal. This middle group is evidently less consistent than those in the extreme positions. However, the differences in neither of the above two questions reach significance.

On all three measures of the fair hiring issue, liberals are found to be more favorable than are conservatives. Table 4-4 shows these results for the ideological positions. Asking whether respondents were in favor of the general principle of fair hiring elicited all but a small minority of positive responses. However, the less general questions refer to friction among present employees when a black was hired to an executive position. These items which involve less outright discrimination find many more respondents opposing fair hiring. Although none of these differences are quite significant, they are consistent in their direction. Respondents who are conservatives again are the most likely to have negative attitudes concerning racial equality.

Questions in the social distance series more or less confirm the by-now-familiar pattern. Liberals are the most positively oriented toward blacks of any subgroup in the entire sample. The last two items show significant differences and the party item is nearly significant. With the exception of the middle-of-the-roaders, who appear to be as likely (perhaps slightly more likely) as liberals to not mind contact with blacks at a party, the pattern is close to what we might have expected. Certainly there seems to be a threshold in interracial contacts which is realized at some point between contact at a party and interaction on more intimate terms. Most strikingly, if we consider the positive responses, liberals (41 percent) are nearly five times as likely as conservatives (9 percent) to be open-minded about a relative dating a black, and nearly four times as likely to accept interracial marriage involving a relative, some 34 percent to 7 percent.

Similar but not significant results were found when respondents were asked whether they actually ever got together socially with blacks (N=152). Again liberals (41 percent) were found to be more likely than conservatives (28 percent) to interact with blacks. Middle-of-the-roaders (19 percent) however, are the least likely to have social contact with blacks.

In sum, the evidence on racial attitudes is relatively clear if not striking. Liberals tend to be more favorable, while conservatives tend to be less favorable on series of questions regarding housing, fair hiring, and interracial contact. Further, there is a consistent tendency for the liberal group to express a greater

**Table 4-4**
**Position on Liberalism-Conservatism Dimension, Fair Hiring Attitudes, and Expression of Social Distance**

| Position | Fair Hiring Question | | | Situations | | |
| | Should Personnel Manager Refuse to Hire Black to Avoid Friction | Should Personnel Manager Ask Employees Whether to Hire Black | Should Employers in General Hire Men Regardless of Race | Party with Blacks | Relative Date Black | Relative Marry Black |
| | Percent Yes | Percent Yes | Percent No | Percent Who Object To | Percent Who Object To | Percent Who Object To |
| Liberal | 27 | 37 | 5 | 17 | 59 | 66 |
| Middle | 35 | 48 | 10 | 15 | 85 | 82 |
| Conservative | 48 | 59 | 18 | 28 | 91 | 93 |

Note: Percentaging is done by rows. Due to differences in missing data the total N ranges from 143-152.

appreciation of the disadvantages faced by blacks. We also found that liberal respondents tend to be less willing to curtail personal freedom as revealed by questions on civil liberties. The data demonstrate that position on the liberalism-conservatism dimension is associated with differences in attitudes among the respondents. Those respondents who see themselves as occupying a position to the left of both major parties are consistently the most liberal on a large number of measures.

## The Liberalism-Conservatism Dimension
## and Personality Characteristics

With regard to personality characteristics there are hardly any differences worth reporting when looking at respondents in nonorganizational positions. However, if we go on to include organizational partisans, an interesting contrast is obvious. While none of these differences can be argued to be statistically significant, we feel that since it is possible to relate this discussion to a body of theory, and since these results—however tentatively—point to an important regularity, our effort is worthwhile.

Table 4-5 shows how the ideological positions compare on three indices of personality measures. There were no apparent differences on misanthropy. The uniformity of liberals, middle-of-the-roaders and conservatives is striking. On the other hand, the organizational partisans are consistently the most negative on these measures, the most notable difference being on dogmatism.

In further support of this distinction, we present in Table 4-5 responses on the stereotype items. Those in nonorganizational positions are generally alike in their rejection of racial traits. Whereas in regard to items on having ambition, being stubborn, and taking care of one's family, organizational partisans are the most likely to accept the validity of these stereotypes. On two of the remaining three items, regarding morals and violence, organizational Republicans are the least likely to believe in the equality of the races. The item on perception of sports ability finds organizational Democrats most in agreement with the existence of a racial trait.

We may submit in conjunction with results on the dogmatism index that these findings indicate a more general predisposition on the part of organizational partisans to be closed-minded. How might we explain this predisposition?

We should consider the possibility that some personality types are strongly attracted to a party, any party, as a group. Returning to Table 2-7 we find that organizational partisans, whether they place themselves relative to one party or the other, are very likely to identify as strong partisans.

In Table 4-5 we have looked at the predisposition of organizational partisans to be closed-minded, and not examined the question of the closed-minded being attracted to the organizational positions. In fact, organizational partisans are overrepresented among the high dogmatics by some 100 percent!

**Table 4-5**
**Position on the Liberalism-Conservatism Dimension, Personality Measures, and Stereotyping**

| | Personality Measures | | | Stereotyping of Racial Traits | | | | | |
| | Percent Agreeing to All Questions on | | | Percent About Equally True of Blacks and Whites | | | | | |
| Position | Fascism | Dogmatism | Social Recognition | Good in Sports | Inclined Toward Violence | High Ambition | High Morals | Being Stubborn | Taking Care of One's Family |
|---|---|---|---|---|---|---|---|---|---|
| Liberal | 35 | 29 | 9 | 76 | 61 | 24 | 56 | 83 | 51 |
| Democrat | 70 | 50 | 25 | 50 | 80 | 20 | 50 | 50 | 30 |
| Middle | 35 | 21 | 9 | 67 | 61 | 44 | 56 | 67 | 52 |
| Republican | 53 | 47 | 20 | 73 | 33 | 7 | 27 | 52 | 27 |
| Conservative | 48 | 27 | 7 | 72 | 49 | 28 | 37 | 73 | 51 |

Note: Percentaging is done by rows. Due to missing data the total N varies from 170-177.

The previous data on social background, public views, and personality demonstrates that positions along the liberalism-conservatism dimension differ in several areas. The appearance of a general left-right pattern among the ideologues confirms the meaningfulness of the liberalism-conservatism continuum for these respondents. The chief exception to this pattern are those in organizational positions who are frequently found to be the most conservative in their attitudes across issue arenas as well as somewhat more likely to be attracted to the political party qua group and to be closed-minded. This deviation suggests the need for a modification in the conventional left-right continuum.

# 5

## The Emerging Independent

### Introduction

We now depart somewhat from our analysis of ideologues and turn to an underlying concern, the position of the Independent in our political system, our central interest being the manner in which respondents relate themselves to this system. It will be recalled that Independents are not found to be the least ideological element of the sample. Moreover, when considering the political spectrum of seven major positions, we found a less than uniform pattern among the three groups of Independents (Table 2-2). Rather, a curvilinear pattern is obvious with the Independents of partisan leaning being much more likely than Independents of no leaning to recognize ideological labels.

Among those Independents who are ideologues there is also a marked variability (Table 2-6). The majority of Independents do not place themselves in the middle of the liberalism-conservatism continuum, although a large plurality of Democratic leaners place themselves in this position. Those leaning to the right are considerably more likely than those leaning to the left to occupy a position on the liberalism-conservatism dimension that is consistent with their partisan leanings.

The ability to relate oneself to the major parties surely taps the respondent's level of awareness. Since Independents as a group are more likely than Democrats to be ideologues, this suggests that Independents have more consistent political attitudes.

### The Conventional Image of the Independent

The common image of the Independent is a rather unflattering one. Campbell et al. (1960) find that generally the stronger the association to the party, the greater is the psychological involvement in political affairs. Specifically, regarding Independents they conclude that:

Far from being more attentive, interested, and informed, Independents tend as a group to be somewhat less involved in politics. They have somewhat poorer knowledge of the issues, their image of the candidates is fainter, their interest in the campaign is less, their concern over the outcome is relatively slight, and their choice between competing candidates, although it is indeed made later in the campaign, seems much less to spring from discoverable evaluations of the elements of national politics (Campbell et al., 1960:143).

Thus, Campbell et al. (1960) fall into a tradition of conceiving of the Independent as the least articulate voter (Campbell et al., 1954; Lazarsfeld et al., 1944). As Shapiro (1969:117) writes, "Systematic voting behavior studies over the past few decades have consistently indicated that the independent voter tends to be relatively uninformed and inattentive to political matters." Strong partisanship, on the other hand, is considered to correlate positively with knowledge of politics (Milbrath, 1965).

Most studies done since Campbell et al. (1960), have merely echoed without questioning this image of the Independent. Writing in 1969 one political commentator argues as follows:

Moreover, the image of the Independent as the superior, rational voter is nonsensical. On every criteria [sic] of voting performance that can be devised, the Independents are vastly inferior to partisans. Independents have poorer knowledge of the issues and candidates, have a lower interest in the campaign and its outcome, make their choice later and with less rationale, and are less likely to vote at all. The more partisan the voter, the more likely he is to have the positive attributes of the good citizen voter. *Independents are the least informed, rational, and participant part of the electorate* (James, 1969:86). (Italics mine.)[1]

The "primary reason" for the inferiority of the Independents is that "partisanship gives a voter stronger motivation to participate and therefore a greater probability of being informed. . . . Either way, partisans are underrated as voters" (James, 1969:87). It sounds as if this author sees partisanship as a necessary if not sufficient motivational basis for political awareness.

Underlining the paucity of alternative discussions of the Independent is the lack of consideration of the possibility that Independents occupy positions more extreme than that of the strong partisans.[2] By way of illustration, we quote from a recent discussion of partisan divisions:

Campaigns increase the relative percentage of strong partisans and after the campaign is over many voters *slide back* to being weak partisans or Independents leaning in one direction. Moreover, equal shifts from one party to the other or to Independents, or vice versa, would cancel each other out leaving no net changes, despite a great deal of redistribution of voters. This is, in fact, what happens. The exact percentage is difficult to establish, but at any given time roughly 20 percent of *the electorate has shifted from one party to the other or to the Independents, or has moved away from the Independents* to one of the major parties. Roughly half of this change has occurred in the last four-year period between one Presidential campaign and the next. The electorate is like a pack of cards that gets partially reshuffled from one election to another. *Strong partisans provide relatively stable cores, but the weak partisans and Independents are in flux.* This permits more movement and potential for change than the raw figures would imply (James, 1969:85). (Italics mine.)

Here Independents are assumed to be exclusively middle-of-the-roaders redistributed every election between the strong partisan positions which serve as "stable cores." Voters beyond the strong partisans also add to the redistribution of votes, but in a manner which no one has yet fully documented.[3]

Independents then, have been seen conventionally as positioned *between* the Democratic and Republican parties. The Independents are said to be pulled to the left to support the Democrats or to the right in support of the Republicans, or split and, therefore shared more or less equally by the major parties. However, our data indicate that the variation in the political system is not bounded simply by strong partisan positions. There are respondents who identify themselves as Independent, and who occupy positions to the *right of right* or to the *left of left* (see Table 2-5).[4] The notion that there is a single relevant dimension bounded by strong partisan positions can be seen as an overly simplified description of our political system.

Only by acknowledging that some Independents are *beyond* the scope of the traditional liberalism-conservatism spectrum, and thus asking about the voters of all orientations who are right of right, and left of left, can we fully account for the fluidity, the ebb and flow of the political system. The evidence suggests that there is not simply a single pool of Independents which the major parties may draw upon. The Democratic and Republican parties are not only competing for the same centralized group of voters, but each party also is competing for an extreme group. If it is not successful in this latter competition, the citizens "beyond the poles" may not vote. The members of the electorate who are left of left and right of right, beyond the bounded linear dimension, are not generally treated by survey research studies.[5]

## Independents and the Political Parties

Were Independents to play the role of "floating voters" providing some slack between the Democratic and Republican parties, we would expect to find (a) that Independents would tend to lean toward one of the major parties or the other, and (b) that in the aggregate, they would tend to regard themselves as more conservative than the Democratic party but more liberal than the Republican party. Indeed, the ISR electoral series reveals that through the 1950s, an Independent was as likely to regard himself as leaning toward a particular political party as he was to see himself as completely unaligned. In the 1960s however, at the national level, the unaligned Independent, with no partisan leanings, was emerging as the modal type (see Table 2-1). Our 1969 Detroit data show 45 percent of our Independents indicating no leaning toward either major party. This might be regarded as a manifestation of the weakening linkage between the two major American parties and the American electorate of the late 1960s. Another manifestation of this phenomenon in our 1969 Detroit data was that among those respondents who identified with a political party, those who saw themselves as weak supporters of that party outnumbered strong supporters by a ratio of almost 2:1 (Table 2-1).

Among those Independents who place themselves ideologically with regard to the two major parties, there is not a strong tendency to adopt a middle-of-the-road position. As Table 2-6 reveals, those with no partisan leaning are most likely to see themselves as more liberal than both parties, and next most likely to see themselves as more conservative than both parties. Rather than serving as a floating vote between the major parties, these voters might well serve as bases of support for third parties at both political extremes. Indeed, while the plurality of independents leaning toward the Democratic party who placed themselves on a liberalism-conservatism continuum saw their political positions as more conservative than the Democratic party but more liberal than the Republican party, slightly more than one-third saw themselves as more conservative than both major parties. A group of independent voters who are going to have to make a choice between the Republican party and the American Independent party will have a different effect on the issue positions taken by the Republican party than will a group of independent voters choosing between the Democratic and Republican parties.

Referring to the supposed characteristics of inarticulateness and indifference, some theorists regard the middle-of-the-road political independent as *functional* for the political system. Berelson et al. (1954), for example, write:

Low affects toward the election—not caring much—underlies the resolution of many political problems. . . . Low interest provides maneuvering room for political shifts necessary for a complex society in a period of rapid change (p. 314). . . . Curiously, the voters least admirable when measured against individual requirements contribute most when measured against the aggregate requirement for flexibility. . . . Without them—if the decision were left only to the deeply concerned, well-integrated, consistently principled ideal citizens—the political system might easily prove too rigid to adapt to changing domestic and international conditions (p. 316).

In this view, the low degree of involvement and of ideological commitment that Berelson and his colleagues saw characterizing most American voters, and which have more recently been assumed to characterize political independents in particular, make positive contributions to the short term flexibility and long term stability of the American two party system. Independents, by serving as a "floating vote" between the Democratic and Republican parties, prevent elections from being wholly determined by rigid partisan alignments. Rather, factors that effect the division of the vote of people who are not committed partisans can have a major impact on electoral outcomes. Among these factors, presumably, is the ability of the parties to present the electorate with platforms that indicate adaptability to changing conditions.

## The Changing Image of the Political Independent

During the last decade, the image of the Independent as uninformed, disinterested, and uninvolved, has been challenged on at least two occasions. Converse (1964) is perhaps the first investigator to formally question the undifferentiated image of the Independent. As he suggests (1964:227), "one of the most intriguing findings . . . [is that] among the most highly sophisticated, those who consider themselves 'Independents' outnumber those who consider themselves 'strong' partisans. . . ." For Converse this finding has two major implications, both of which fit into our framework. The party as a group is "likely to have less centrality in the belief systems of the most sophisticated . . . the centrality of group as referents increases lower down in the sophistication ordering" (Converse, 1964:227). Moreover, "we see in this reversal at least a partial explanation of the old assumption that the independent voter is relatively informed and involved" (Converse, 1964:227). That this image has rarely been espoused, Converse attributes partly to the situation that other studies have so often substantiated the picture of an uninformed and uninvolved Independent "that it is hard to imagine how any opposing perception could have developed" (Converse, 1964:227). Surely, we could suggest that the image of the Independent as the least informed is partially a result of the selective nature of earlier studies.

Converse summarizes a study by Flanigan (1961), comparing Independent voters with strong partisans, as follows: "Some of the customary findings relating political independence with low involvement and low information then became blurred or in some cases reversed themselves altogether. Our highly sophisticated independents contribute to this phenomenon" (Converse, 1964:257fn). The undifferentiated treatment of Independents can be traced back from the early major contributions to the contemporary image. There is very little of alternative discussions.

However, we must not overlook research in the field of political socialization. This research suggests that political party choice is most generally transmitted from parent to child, and that the child develops an affective attachment to his parents' party as a political object (Langton, 1969:53). Hess and Torney (1968:97) report that as children age, they believe less and less in family loyalty as an appropriate basis for deciding which party to support, However, even these authors concede that where the parents agree on party choice, their children will follow their lead 75 percent of the time. What makes this figure more remarkable is that family loyalty persists as a factor of central importance in the face of ideological differences between generations. What seems to happen is that the child, having developed an affective attachment to a party as a political object, then derives from contemporary political events a series of justifications for his party choice (cf. Hyman, 1959:74). He therefore agrees with his parents' choice of political party, but has different specific reasons for that choice than they do.

The rarity of major political realignments in the American electorate attests to the strength of the ties between voters and their parties.[6] While there is some ticket splitting, and partisans of one persuasion sometimes vote for candidates of the other, one does not frequently find large numbers of voters severing their emotional links to one party, and establishing links with another. When such realignments do take place, moreover, they seem to occur over an extended period of time (V.O. Key, 1958; Sellers, 1965). It appears to be easier for a Democrat to become a nonDemocrat than for him to become a Republican. Thus, during realignment phases, third-party movements may play an important role as "half-way houses," giving expartisans of one major persuasion a political object on which to roost while getting accustomed to the idea of supporting the party that in their youth was defined as the opposition (MacRae and Neldrum, 1960; Alford, 1963:287-308).

Where does this leave us in regard to the Independent? The fact of political socialization occurring in childhood provides us with one theoretical basis for criticism of the contemporary portrayal of Independents. In support of our belief in the desirability of modifying the conventional image of the Independent, we turn to the monumental work by Hess and Torney (1968).

Party affiliation is most often acquired by the later years of elementary school, and Hess and Torney (1968:101) find "the proportion of children who report that they would vote independently of partisan affiliation is large and increases with age." It is especially interesting that the proportion of school children who these authors find to report political independence (32 percent) is quite similar to the size of the Independent group among the voting population (1968:102). The children of Independents were frequently found to be Independents. Apparently independence and party attachment are acquired through a *similar* process of identification with an adult figure.

For the voting population, education is directly related to political participation (Campbell et al., 1960). Similarly, in children it is intelligence that is central to the acquisition of political attitudes. "High intelligence accelerates the acquisition of political attitudes" (Hess and Torney, 1968:148), and Hess and Torney's data reveal that children who report independence are both highly intelligent, and most often come from high status backgrounds. Thus, it is not surprising when they conclude that, "Children who are independent of party show the most active involvement in political affairs" (1968:231). It is the independent group, they argue, which "most closely approximate[s] the image of the independent, thoughtful voter who is informed on issues and chooses his candidate after careful reflection" (Hess and Torney, 1968:232). These data provide at least partial confirmation for the need to alter the image of partisans as politically more aware than Independents.

On the basis of available evidence, we must include ourselves among the ranks of those who feel, first, that the traditional apolitical image of the Independent is not applicable to large numbers of voters who consider themselves Independents, and second, that because of the level of political involvement of these Independents, they are unlikely to play the "floating voter" role of mediation between the two major political parties that Berelson et al., among others, assigned to them.

## Independence, Awareness, and
## Social Background

Our inquiry now leads us to a consideration of whether the high intelligence and high status backgrounds of children who are independent of party is paralleled by high educational attainment and high status characteristics among Independents in the Detroit electorate. We do not find significant differences in social background characteristics between people who regard themselves as Independents and those who identify with a political party. However, when we disaggregate the partisans into Republicans and Democrats, the latter are significantly lower on all measures of status, and the Independents tend to fall between the two groups of partisans.

In Table 5-1 we present the results of political identification against select background variables. On all measures of SES, with the exception of home ownership, Independents lie between Republicans, who are of generally higher status characteristics and Democrats, characterized generally by lower status. It is apparent that as a group Independents are not of the highest social strata. However, we demonstrated in Table 2-2 that Independents are by no means an undifferentiated group. The Independents of no leaning pull the entire group of Independents in a less ideological direction.

In their own right, Independents are more likely than Democrats to be of high occupational status. Moreover, the likelihood of greater political awareness on the part of Independents relative to Democrats is implied by the finding that Independents are more than twice as likely as Democrats to have completed a college education. On this basis we would expect Independents to be more politically aware than Democratic identifiers.

While Independents are a middle group in occupational, educational, and financial status measures, they break this pattern on other measures. The data indicate that among those not born and raised in Detroit, Independents are considerably more likely than members of both partisan positions to have been born and raised in a large city. We know that citizens in urbanized environments tend to be more politically active or aware (Berelson et al., 1954; Campbell,

**Table 5-1**
**Political Identification by Select Background Factors**

| Political Identification | Occupation Percent Professional, Technical and Managerial | Education Percent Some College+ | Father's Education Percent Some College+ | Family Income Percent $17,000+ | Age Percent 18-39 | 60+ | Sex Percent Male | Home Ownership Percent Rent | Religion Prot. | Percent Cath. | Jew | Type of Community Raised in as Child Percent Large City |
|---|---|---|---|---|---|---|---|---|---|---|---|---|
| Republican (142) | 49 | 53 | 21 | 25 | 38 | 19 | 44 | 13 | 77 | 17 | 1 | 25 |
| Democrat (285) | 20 | 14 | 5 | 9 | 40 | 12 | 45 | 16 | 36 | 58 | 2 | 29 |
| Independent (199) | 32 | 32 | 16 | 14 | 52 | 8 | 55 | 21 | 46 | 42 | 3 | 39 |
| Total (626) | 30 | 29 | 12 | 14 | 44 | 12 | 48 | 17 | 49 | 43 | 2 | 31 |

Note: The N for type of community raised in as a child is only 323.

1962; Campbell et al., 1964; Lazarsfeld et al., 1944; Rokkan and Campbell, 1960). Therefore, one would likely conclude that the evidence seems to favor the political awareness of the Independent.

Further, Independents are disproportionately young–the most likely to be under forty years and the least likely to be over sixty years. Once a voting pattern is reinforced by time it is likely to become stabilized, so that partisan identification tends to increase gradually with age, while Independence declines. As Milbrath (1965:53) suggests, "Older persons tend to have stronger party preferences than younger." He explains the variation in political awareness in relation to the life cycle. "The most apathetic group are the young, unmarried citizens who are only marginally integrated into their community" (Milbrath, 1965:134). Independents seem to be less firmly attached to the system than partisans. They are the most likely to be young, twice as likely to be unmarried, and the most likely to rent rather than own a house.[7] The data on education suggest the desirability of modifying the argument that the relationship between age and commitment to a major political party necessarily means that the Independent is less politically aware.

Another related and distinctive characteristic of Independents is their sex. They are the only group with a majority of men. Thus, we can see the overrepresentation of men among the Independent group as a further promising finding that questions the supposed lower level of political awareness among Independents. The weight of evidence goes against a simplified conception of the relationship between awareness and partisanship.

Religious differences in political identification are apparent. While Independents are nearly balanced between the two major religious groupings in our society, over three-fourths of Republicans are Protestant, and nearly three-fifths of Democrats are of the Catholic faith. The marked overrepresentation of Catholics in Detroit was noted earlier (see Table 1 1). Although the political consequences of religion are minimal (Milbrath, 1965:137), this overrepresentation among Democrats of Catholics may interact with ethnicity and the strength of local unionization, thus having an impact on political involvement.

In order to add to our investigation of the political awareness of Independents, we looked for differences in "don't know" rates as we did for ideologues and nonideologues. However, there were few apparent differences in mention of "don't know" responses. This being the case we restricted ourselves to a consideration of interview items which indicate level of awareness.

On questions ascertaining the respondent's appreciation of racial discrimination there are no significant differences. However, Democratic identifiers without exception appear to be somewhat less aware than Republicans and Independents of black disadvantages. For example, some 17 percent of Independents, 13 percent of Republicans, and 10 percent of Democrats believe that there is a lot of job discrimination in the Detroit area.

The three political groups do differ significantly on the issue of how to prevent a riot from recurring. Independents are nearly twice as likely as Democrats and half again as likely as Republicans to opt for improving the social and economic conditions of blacks. Perhaps it is reasonable to assume that those who are more aware would see the need for dealing with conditions which promote racial disorders.

*The Size of the Independent Group*

There is one possibility that might allow us to reconcile the alternate images of the Independent. The more aware Independent may represent today an *increasing* proportion of those identifying themselves as Independents. It is interesting to entertain the possibility that the meaning of political independence has changed. This possibility suggests that earlier studies were accurate in their representations of the Independent. The overwhelming majority of Independents in the 1940s and 1950s may indeed have been the least sophisticated members of the electorate, while those identifying with a party might have been more aware. Certainly there does seem to be a general increase in the numbers, and fashionability, of Independents.

This leads us to a consideration of whether we have an atypically large number of Independents in our sample. Such an overrepresentation of Independents would suggest the existence of certain localized social conditions prompting the rejection of partisanship. A comparison with the 1968 Survey Research Center Election Study (see Table 1-1) shows this reservation to be unfounded. Our sample closely resembles the national figures, being some 2 percent higher in Independents. This difference can probably be accounted for by the higher proportion of young people in the Detroit Area Study sample, and also urban-rural differences in the samples.

In this regard, data from the 1968 Survey Research Center study concerning party identification in cities of 50,000 and up is relevant. Thirty-nine percent of respondents identify themselves as Independent, as compared to 22 percent Republican and 39 percent Democrat. In this light, the proportion of our sample claiming to be Independents is not surprising. The Survey Research Center reported that 48 percent of their respondents aged 21 to 29 were Independent. Other sources similarly indicate a large percent of Independents.[8]

Moreover, there does seem to have been over time an increase in the proportion of Independent identifiers. In 1960 a Survey Research Center study recorded 23 percent Independent. This compares to the 29 percent found in 1968. The proportion of Independents now seems to be at an all time high point (Table 5-2).[9]

The war in Vietnam, in conjunction with other major developments in the 1960s and early 1970s, has created dissatisfaction with the party system among segments of the electorate. There is reason to believe, from such developments as

**Table 5-2**
**Variation in Partisan Identification: 1952-1968**

| Partisan Identification | High | Low (Percent) | Median |
|---|---|---|---|
| Democratic | 51 | 45 | 46 |
| Republican | 29 | 24 | 27 |
| Independent | 29 | 19 | 24 |
| Apolitical | 5 | 1 | 3 |

Source: Simplification of data presented by Survey Research Center, *The Distribution of Party Identification in the United States* (Ann Arbor, Michigan: The University of Michigan, Mimeograph, November 1968).

the Wallace phenomena and the New Left, that this dissatisfaction transcends age group boundaries. The reluctance of many party leaders to respond to central problems has apparently undermined for some the legitimacy and credibility of the present system. More and more, Independents can be seen as protest voters. In sum, there are reasons to suspect that political independence isn't what it used to be, such as an increase in respectability, in size, and changes in motivational bases.

By investigating the Independent in our political system we are acknowledging the fact that the major task of the political parties is not to attract voters of the opposite persuasion to vote for them, but to appeal to uncommitted voters. Given the emotional ties that exist between voters and parties, elections tend not to be won on the basis of one party attracting supporters of the opposite persuasion to its cause (Segal, 1968). Rather, the electoral task of each party is to get its own partisans to the polls, and to maximize its attractiveness to Independent voters. In the current American electorate, the Democrats have a plurality, but due largely to socioeconomic differences, Republican voters are more likely to go to the polls. In our political system, then, the role of the Independent becomes crucial. The pivotal position of Independents is demonstrated by the results of the 1968 election which was decided by 300,000 out of 73,000,000 votes.

To sum up, the data on the increase of political independence and the backgrounds of independents must be viewed in the context of a previously demonstrated positive relationship between social status and political involvement (see for example Campbell et al., 1960), and "inflation" of the status structure in the United States (Segal and Felson, 1973; Duncan, 1965). While we cannot draw direct inferences from aggregate data and trends, we certainly have a basis for questioning both the lower social status of political independents and their hypothesized lower rates of political involvement.

### Independent Ideologues and Issue Orientations

Up to this point our analysis has involved variation along two major dimensions, those of partisanship and ideology. Here we bring together our interests in these distinct dimensions for a consideration of Independent ideologues. The common portrayal of the Independent suggests that he or she does not really have a set of political attitudes. In contrast, evidence has been presented for modifying this image of the Independent in our political system. Converse suggests that Independents are overrepresented among ideological voters. Also we have considered differences between respondents who are able to use the terms "liberal" and "conservative" and those who do not appear to recognize these concepts, finding that ideologues are apparently both more aware and sophisticated than nonideologues. Our purpose here is to focus briefly on left-right differences among the Independent subsample.

To gather evidence on Independents, we decided to employ the most stringent measure of liberalism-conservatism (see Table 2-6 and Figure 2-2). We may tentatively define Independents who placed themselves *consistently* on a liberalism-conservatism continuum relative to both major parties as independent ideologues, and then determine (a) whether they took positions on political issues, and (b) whether these positions were consistent with their placement on the liberalism-conservatism dimension. Of the 177 ideologues, 140 were consistent as to party and position. There are 42 Independents among this subsample: 13 left Independents, 18 centrists, and 11 right Independents. The major difficulty with the analysis in this section is the small number of cases available. We will rely on percentage differences, not on $Chi^2$, the number of expected cases often being too few for significance testing. Only a high level of consistency in our results can make this meaningful.

The responses of the three groups of Independents are quite distinct. The distribution of attitudes tends to follow the pattern of increasing liberalism from right to left. However, as is the case for the larger group of ideologues, the Independents do not seem to differ on issues of social welfare.

The results on civil liberties and civil rights issues are revealing. Though the Ns are small, the consistency of the left-right pattern holding over a number of measures makes the results noteworthy. In Table 5-3 we compare the results of the Independents and our total sample on three measures of civil liberties. The pattern of *increasing liberalism* right-to-left holds in all cases. It is especially interesting that not one of the rightists opposes the use of wiretapping by police. Moreover, on the wiretapping question the percent of conditional answers is the same for all categories, implying a uniformity in the predisposition of Independent ideologues to volunteer more sophisticated responses. The results on the questions of banning movies in which nude actors appear and the threat posed by Communists are practically identical. This similarity may indicate that Independent ideologues see a general theme of social change underlying these

**Table 5-3**

**Comparing Independent Ideologues to the Total Sample (Responses on Civil Liberties Issues)**

| | Civil Liberties Issues | | | | | | | |
| | Police Wiretap Telephone % | | | Ban Movies with Nude Actors % | | Communist Danger % | | % |
| Position | Yes | Yes, But | No | Yes | No | Great | Less | Total |
|---|---|---|---|---|---|---|---|---|
| Left (N=13) | 38 | 16 | 46 | 23 | 77 | 23 | 77 | 100 |
| Centrist (N=18) | 55 | 17 | 28 | 41 | 59 | 39 | 61 | 100 |
| Right (N=11) | 82 | 18 | 0 | 55 | 45 | 55 | 45 | 100 |
| Total (N=42) | 57 | 17 | 26 | 39 | 61 | 38 | 62 | 100 |
| Total Sample (N=626) | 76 | 4 | 20 | 48 | 52 | 47 | 53 | 100 |

questions. Finally, we can observe that while as a group Independent ideologues tend to be more liberal than the overall sample, the rightists are the *least* liberal subgroup of the entire sample. That is to say, among the Independent ideologue subgroup we find the most extreme respondents. Related to the civil liberties questions we also find that leftists are the least likely to favor white "vigilante" groups. However, the differences are not sharp here.

A pair of questions not previously found to differ between ideologues or nonideologues involves attitudes on city ordinances. Respondents were asked whether there should be city laws requiring property owners "to keep their lawns cut to a reasonable level," and "to keep junk out of their back yard." A three point index was constructed on these orientations toward city ordinances. The "none" category includes those who oppose both laws, while the second category includes those who favor one law or the other, and the final category is comprised of respondents who support both laws (Table 5-4). By this evidence rightists overwhelmingly tend to favor city and property laws. A "law and order" orientation increasing from left to right seems to be suggested by the results on civil liberties issues and related items.

Moving on to the civil rights area, there are no apparent differences in awareness of the social and economic disadvantages with which blacks are confronted. Since we are looking at a select group of ideologues, it is perhaps easy to understand why there is a uniformity in perception of black disadvantages. However, we do encounter a left-right pattern on answers to the question of how to prevent another racial riot from occurring (N=42). Some 38 percent of leftists stress repressive action such as "police power," "enforced curfew," "harsh treatment for offenders," while 56 percent of the centrists, and 72 percent of rightists mention such negative solutions.

**Table 5-4**

**Independent Ideologues, Support of City Property Laws, and Expression of Racial Distance Toward Blacks (N=42)**

| | City Property Laws | | | Social Distance Situations | | |
|---|---|---|---|---|---|---|
| | Grass Cutting and Garbage Removal | | | Party with Blacks Present | Relative Date Black | Relative Marry Black |
| Position | Percent Support None | Percent Support One | Percent Support Two | Percent Object To | Percent Object To | Percent Object To |
| Left (13) | 15 | 39 | 46 | – | 31 | 38 |
| Center (18) | 11 | 28 | 61 | 17 | 83 | 83 |
| Right (11) | – | 9 | 91 | 64 | 91 | 91 |

Note: Percentaging is done by rows.

Measures of the action component of attitudes similarly indicate that the right is "hard," and the left is "soft" in their racial attitudes. One of the more distinctive measures is selling one's house to a black couple. Willingness to sell one's house to a black couple is highest among the leftists, (fully 85 percent), lower among the centrists (some 56 percent), and very much lower among the rightists, (only 27 percent). On the community-wide housing issue vote, rightists (9 percent) are only one-third as likely as both centrists (33 percent) and leftists (31 percent) to support open housing. Further, rightists are the most likely to have moved out because blacks were moving into their neighborhood. Relatedly, some 70 percent of leftists would support a bussing proposal, while only 45 percent of the rightists would support such a proposal.

Social distance items reinforce the image of increasing liberalism right to left. The marked results, surprisingly similar to responses on property law issues, are also presented in Table 5-4 for purposes of comparison. While not a single leftist would object to being at a party where blacks were present, 64 percent of the rightists express a negative reaction. While the centrists are closer to the leftists on this item, the distance between the leftists and the two other groups is obvious in regard to the more intimate items of a relative's dating or marrying a black. Centrists are closer to the right than to the left. The distinctiveness of the leftists' beliefs appears again and again. Thus there is some reason then to suspect that the psychological distance from the center to the left is slightly greater than the distance from the center to the right. This tendency, however slight, perhaps relates to the skewness of the political system toward the right. We may suggest that it would be less "costly" for the major parties to try to attract the rightists who appear to have been inculcated with dominant social values.

Another indirect measure of social distance is the item concerning respondent perception of the residential desires of blacks. While only 23 percent of the leftists think that most blacks prefer segregated residential area, 56 percent of the centrists, and 73 percent of the rightists believe blacks prefer segregated to integrated housing. Again, the centrists and the rightists are closer to one another than to the leftists.

*The Social Background of Independent Ideologues*

While we have previously compared the social backgrounds of Independents and partisans, we have not yet discussed the social characteristics of these ideologues. Interestingly, except for education, the ideological position of these Independents do not vary by social status. While there are no Independent ideologues with less than some high school, the leftists (38 percent) are slightly more likely to have a college education or more, compared to the centrists (22 percent) and the rightists (27 percent). Occupation and income do not discriminate among the Independent ideologues. The only other variable on which differences are apparent is sex. Eight-five percent of the leftists are male as compared to 61 percent of the centrists, and 64 percent of the rightists. Perhaps this is an indication that leftists receive more political stimuli.

The personality characteristics of leftists show them to be more open-minded. While only some 17 percent of the leftists (compared to 53 percent of the entire sample) rank high on the "F" index, 35 percent of the centrists, and 45 percent of the rightists rank high. Similarly, leftists (15 percent) are less than half as likely as both centrists (33 percent) and rightists (36 percent) to score high on a dogmatism scale.

The data suggests that Independent ideologues of various positions differ in attitudes, social background, primarily education, and personality characteristics. These results underline the usefulness of a differentiated investigation of Independents.

# 6 A Structural Analysis of Political Belief Systems

## Introduction

In this chapter the data on ideologues and nonideologues will be examined to see whether or not they reveal different structures for these two groups. Seemingly countless numbers of research studies have attempted to determine whether the electorate has a general left-right issue orientation or whether we must expect their attitudes to vary in different areas. Traditionally, one of the key methods has been the application of factor analysis (Sanai, 1950; Ferguson, 1939, 1940, 1944; Kerr, 1944, 1952; Lentz, 1950; Eysenck, 1954). Almost without exception the major factor isolated has been a general liberalism-conservatism dimension (Olsen, 1962).

However, there is considerable evidence in our data to suggest that the liberalism-conservatism dimension is inadequate as a descriptive mechanism for the attitudes of the public. Many other investigators have also questioned this dimension. For example, Kerr found the average correlation among political, economic, religious, and social attitudes to be about .15, and concludes that the liberal or the conservative is an hypothetical individual who does not exist (Kerr, 1952). Similarly, Eysenck (1954) demonstrates that attitude structure is far too complex for a single dimension. In a now near-classic discussion, Lipset first (1963) distinguished between types of liberalism—economic and noneconomic. Lenski (1963) find religious liberalism or conservatism to bear little relationship to attitudes in other areas. Further, Campbell et al. (1960) show that foreign and domestic policy attitudes are not related. Summing up previous research, Fishel (1969) concludes that the liberalism-conservatism abstraction is not a reliable measure for predicting the attitudes of most Americans and suggests that we turn away from our preoccupation with unidimensionality.

If the liberalism-conservatism dimension is not so common, what frames of reference for ordering issue concerns do enjoy more widespread use? Campbell et al. suggest that

... there must be surrogates for ideology that bring large aggregates to act as though propelled by ideological concerns. It is important to understand the character of these surrogates not only to satisfy intellectual curiosity, but also because the fact that they are surrogates rather than full-blown ideology may from time to time lead to crucial differences in behavior (Campbell et al., 1960:217-218).

Campbell et al. (1960:215) also desire more research in this direction. As they say,

We have suggested that the types of attitude structure presumed in ideological accounts of political behavior are not very prevalent in the American electorate. Though we could never expect great precision in this matter, it would be convenient to have a firmer sense of how prevalent they are. Further analysis in this direction might also improve our understanding of the various modes of conceptual organization that are brought to bear on matters of policy controversy, in lieu of full-blown ideology. Some estimate of the relative incidence of these modes of concept formation would . . . help to corroborate suspicions expressed in this chapter. . . .

One might expect that our ideologues will be more adequately distributed over a one-dimensional liberalism-conservatism space, and that the nonideologues will have to be placed in a multidimensional space before the organization of their attitudes becomes interpretable. However, we do not preclude the possibility that ideologues have multidimensional attitude structures.

### Smallest Space Analysis

Our interest is in revealing domains underlying the variety of attitudes held by the electorate. For analysis of the structural relations between attitude items we turned to the Guttman-Lingoes series of nonmetric techniques.

Smallest space analysis transforms the information contained in a matrix of correlations into a graphic representation. Attitude items are represented by points in a Euclidean space of two or more dimensions. These points are plotted in the m-dimensional space such that the rank order of the empirical relations is preserved.

The condition that must be satisfied in the conversion of the rank ordering is as follows:

$$\text{Distance AB} < \text{Distance AC}$$
$$\text{when } r_{AB} > r_{AC}.$$

Therefore, the higher the positive correlation between two variables the smaller the distance between the points representing them. When the correlation between the variables is low or nonexistent, the points are farther apart. Finally, when variables are negatively associated, the distance between the corresponding points increases as the negative correlation increases until the points are at opposite ends of the space.

The capabilities of this nonmetric method,[1] as well as its advantages over metric procedures, are more than sufficient to make it attractive to the investigator of belief systems. We are able to consider the structure of the total space, as well as the relations between individual items or between groups of items. There is little or no commitment to a given theoretical bias. One can also bypass a number of questionable assumptions about the underlying distribution, the scaling characteristics of the data, etc., and focus directly on the configurational properties of the data. The data are permitted to "speak for themselves" without imposing restrictions in advance of exploring what, if any, structures are present. Further, a graphic representation is achieved in as few dimensions as possible. A smallest two-dimensional space may be equivalent to a six-dimensional factor analytic space (Guttman and Schlesinger, 1969).

The smallest space program attempts to find the minimum number of dimensions in which the data can be accurately represented. Accuracy is gauged in terms of how well the rank ordering of variables is portrayed; that is, the extent to which the distance between items reflect the correlation between them. The acceptability of a smallest space solution is measured by the coefficient of alienation which varies from 1 to 0. A perfect fit yields a coefficient of 0. Generally, a coefficient of .15 or less is considered as an acceptable representation (Guttman, 1968).[2]

*The Correlation Matrix*

In our desire to investigate the implicit relationships formed by the data, we hoped to include as many items as possible from distinct issue arenas. We relied on three rules for selecting items to be included in the smallest space analysis. Excluded from the analysis were any items with 80 percent or more of the valid responses of the total sample falling into a single category. We felt that it would be of little value to include questions with one sided distributions. Moreover, only where the number of valid cases for a question exceeded two-thirds of the total sample did we include the item.[3] Finally, only items which had been included in the earlier analyses were selected. Thus, we chose twenty-nine variables for this analysis. These items appear below (Table 6-1).

All variables were dichotomized into "liberal" or "conservative" categories. We coded each item as 1 for a liberal and 0 for a conservative response, and then correlated these items with each other using the product moment coefficient. Filtering for the ideologue and nonideologue groups before running the correlations, we had two 29 X 29 matrices of correlations. On an initial visual inspection of the inter-item correlations for both groups we are struck first of all by the small size of most correlations, and secondly by the apparent similarity of ideologues and nonideologues. The low inter-item correlations of the nonideologues is not surprising. However, that correlations are nearly as low for the ideologue group suggests, as we are well aware, that our measure of ideology is not a particularly rigorous one.

In the smallest space analysis a good fit was achieved in a three-dimensional

**Table 6-1**
**Items Used in Smallest Space Analysis**

1. Do you think the federal *government* should in some way provide *jobs* for people who are unemployed and can't find work?

2. Do you think the federal government should guarantee free *medical* and hospital *care* for everyone?

3. Do you think the police should be allowed to *wiretap* telephones and listen in on private conversations when they think it is necessary for collecting evidence to solve crimes?

4. In the past few years some movies have come out in which actors appear with little or no clothes on. Do you think such *movies* should be *banned* for everyone or that adults have a right to see whatever they want?

5. There are a few people in this country who consider themselves Communists. Do you think *Communists* living here in the United States are now a very great *danger*, a great danger, some danger, or hardly any danger?

6. Do you think *unemployment* in the Detroit area is greater among Negroes, greater among whites, or about the same for both?

7. How about the *quality* of *housing* that white people and Negroes have: Is the housing worse for the average Negro family, worse for the average white family, or is there not much difference?

8. Do you think the *quality* of *teachers* in Negro areas of Detroit is better than in white areas, about the same, or worse?

9. Where *Negroes* are *behind* whites in such things as jobs or income or housing, do you think this is mainly due to something about Negroes themselves, or mainly due to the way whites have treated Negroes in the past?

10. How much danger, if any, do you think there is of groups of *Negroes* from the inner city going out to white areas and suburbs to commit violence on whites: Do you think this is a great *danger*, some danger, little danger, or no danger?

11. Some people want to *organize whites* into groups to protect themselves against violence by Negroes. Do you think this is a good idea or not?

12. What do you think is the most important thing the city government in Detroit could do to keep a *riot* like the one in 1967 from breaking out again?

13. Would you say there's a lot of *discrimination* against Negroes when they look for a *job* in the Detroit area or little discrimination?

14. How about buying or renting a *home* in the Detroit area? Would you say there's a lot of *discrimination* against Negroes trying to get a home or little discrimination?

The Following Refers to Questions #15, 16, 17, 18:

Here are some characteristics sometimes mentioned about people. For each one, would you tell me whether it is more true of whites, about equally true of Negroes and whites, or more true of Negroes?

15. Being inclined toward *violence*

16. Having high *ambition*

17. Having high *morals*

18. Taking care of one's *family*

19. Here are some situations where you might have to decide on a particular action. Suppose you owned a house on this block and you wanted to sell it. If a *Negro* couple who could afford it wanted to buy it, would you sell to them if you had a choice?

20. Now reverse the situation. Suppose a close *neighbor* was *selling* his house and he had a Negro customer for it. What would you want him to do: sell to the customer or not sell?

**Table 6-1** (cont.)

21. Suppose there is a community-wide vote on the general *housing* issue. There are two possible laws to vote on:

    *One law* says that a homeowner can decide for himself who to sell his house to, even if he prefers not to sell to Negroes.

    The *second law* says that a homeowner *cannot* refuse to sell to someone because of his race or color.

    Which law would you vote for?

22. Suppose there was a *proposal* at your children's school to give Negro parents an opportunity to transfer in about 25 Negro children from a very over-crowded school. The principal of your school calls a meeting of all parents to decide on the proposal and you go to the meeting. Would you support or oppose the proposal at the meeting?

23. One day a six year old asks her mother if she can bring another girl home to *play*. The mother knows that the other girl is a Negro, and that her own daughter has only played with white children before. What should the mother do?

The Following Refers to Questions #24, 25:

Suppose a good Negro engineer applied for a job as an engineering executive. The Personnel Director explained to him: "Personally, I'd never give your race a thought, but the two men you would have to work with most closely—the plant manager and the chief engineer—both have strong feelings about Negroes. I *can* offer you a job as a regular engineer, but *not* at the executive level, because any serious friction at the top could ruin the organization.

24. Was it all right for the personnel director in this case to refuse to *hire* the *Negro* engineer as an executive in order to avoid friction with other employees?

25. Should the personnel manager have *asked* the other *men* how they would feel about working with a Negro engineer and then made his decision on the basis of their wishes?

The Following Refers to Questions #26, 27, 28:

Now I'd like you to imagine the following things happening. Please tell me how *you* would feel personally, even though you might not object openly.

26. If you went to a *house-party* and discovered that several Negro couples were there would you personally mind a lot, a little, or not at all?

27. If a very close relative went on a *date* with a *Negro*, would you mind a lot, a little, or not at all?

28. If a very close relative *married* a *Negro*, would you mind a lot, a little, or not at all?

29. At present some *Negro* neighborhoods have *schools* with rundown buildings and less trained teachers than schools in mainly white neighborhoods. Do you think the federal government should provide more money to bring those Negro schools up to the standard of the white schools, or that the government shouldn't do this?

solution. The coefficients obtained for ideologues are .43, .29, .20, and for non-ideologues, .42, .26, .18 in 1-3 dimensions respectively. The coefficients are nearly identical for each space, reflecting the similarity of the correlation matrices. There are various explanations, of course, of why we find these coefficients. Most apparently, we are not dealing with a unidimensional space for ideologues; in fact the nonideologues are found to have a slightly better fit in each space. The size of the sample, of course, affects the reliability of the smallest space solution. The larger the sample the less the variability or "noise."

In this case the nonideologues exceed the ideologues by nearly two to one. Thus, the smallest space solution may not be as adequate for the ideologues. The desirability of being able to compare larger subsamples of equal size is obvious.

The coefficients of .20 and .18 are nearly acceptable.[4] Going from a two- to a three-dimensional space however, we do not gain a great deal in the quality of the fit. Inspecting the arrangement of the items in three dimensions we also found the configurations to be basically similar. Thus, the slight increase in the acceptability of the fit in an increased dimension does not warrant focusing on the more complex three-dimensional space. For the sake of parsimony, we feel it is more reasonable to present a two-dimensional than a three-dimensional solution. A two-dimensional space is both easier to visualize and to understand.

## Interpretation of the
## Two-Dimensional Space

The above coefficients suggest, as the data in Chapter 3 did, that ideologues and nonideologues are quite similar. Turning to the arrangements of the twenty-nine items, Figures 6-1 and 6-2 present the space diagrams for ideologues and nonideologues respectively.

The graphic representations of the points portray the patterns of the presence or absence of liberal responses. Our initial efforts at interpreting the space involved thinking of several labels for the principle axes. At first down the right-hand side of the space in Figure 6-1 there seemed to be a dimension of economic liberalism running from education to employment and finally to socialized medicine. Moreover, a variant of a noneconomic liberalism dimension seemed apparent. This dimension also ran up and down, starting with the "open housing" and "bussing proposal" items, which are not directly involved with interracial contact, moving on to the "sell to black" and "neighbor" items, which imply more direct contact, and ending with the social distance items which relate directly to interracial contact. However, these and other initial efforts at labeling dimensions were discarded, as we were not able to clearly isolate such dimensions. Yet there is nothing sacrosanct about the concept of dimension, so we searched for other patterns in the space.

As Figures 6-1 and 6-2 show, there are distinct clusters of items. We outlined these clusters, and designated each by a Roman numeral. These clusters are listed below. There are two bases on which we derived these clusters. Firstly, the points had to be close enough together to indicate that they were positively associated. The simple correlation between any two variables does not by itself determine their relative position since all other points are taken into account. In addition, it was necessary for the points to relate meaningfully to one another on a theoretical basis.

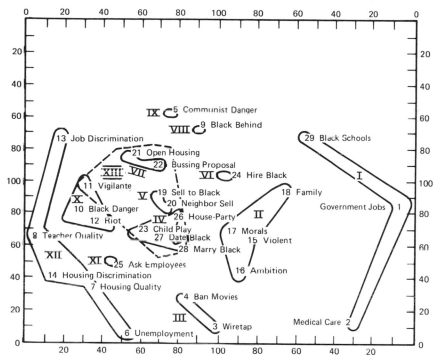

**Figure 6-1.** Smallest Space Diagram for Ideologues (N=177).

Clusters of Items in Figure 6-1.

| | |
|---|---|
| I | Social Welfare |
| II | Racial Traits |
| III | Civil Liberties |
| IV | Social Distance |
| V | Selling House to Black |
| VI | Fair Hiring |
| VII | Legislative Action on Civil Rights |
| VIII | Responsibility for Black Disadvantages |
| IX | Civil Liberties |
| X | Racial Violence |
| XI | Fair Hiring |
| XII | Awareness of Racial Discrimination and Disadvantages of Blacks |
| XIII | Action Component of Racial Attitudes. |

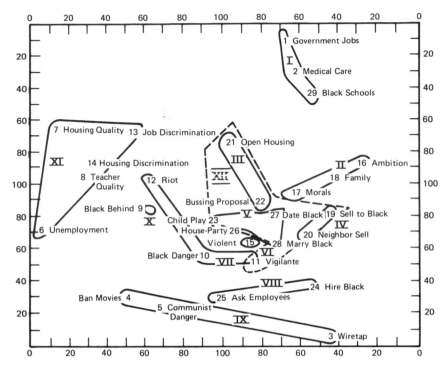

**Figure 6-2.** Smallest Space Diagram for Non-ideologues (N=317).

Clusters of Items in Figure 6-2.

| | |
|---|---|
| I | Social Welfare |
| II | Racial Traits |
| III | Legislative Action on Civil Rights |
| IV | Selling House to Black |
| V | Social Distance |
| VI | Racial Traits |
| VII | Racial Violence |
| VIII | Fair Hiring |
| IX | Civil Liberties |
| X | Responsibility for Black Disadvantages |
| XI | Awareness of Racial Discrimination and Disadvantages of Blacks |
| XII | Action Component of Racial Attitudes |

In the space diagram we see that the clusters which exist are roughly the same for both samples. What differences that are apparent in the contents of clusters involve only three items: 5, 15, and 24. For the nonideologues, point 5, referring to the danger posed by Communists, and point 24, relating to the hiring of a black engineer, are closer respectively to similar civil liberties and fair hiring items than is the case for ideologues. On the other hand, while we find item 15 to fall into a fairly tight social distance cluster among the ideologue group, it does not do so for the nonideologues.

Let us first consider the relations between the variables within the clusters. In the social welfare cluster the correlations are about the same for both groups. The correlations among the social welfare responses are presented in Table 6-2. The average correlation is somewhat higher for the nonideologues.

Instead of presenting a large number of tables detailing the correlations for items within clusters, we present Table 6-3. This table gives the average interitem correlation within each cluster for both groups. Bearing in mind that due to its smaller N a higher correlation is necessary for significance among the ideologue group, we find that in only one instance is the average correlation for the ideologues notably higher.

The highest correlations for each group exist between attitudes towards selling a house to blacks, fair hiring, and social distance items. There are four items included in the social distance cluster, and since many of the other items show a significant positive association with them, the social distance items appear to occupy central locations. Significantly high correlations exist between action items, implying a consistency in regard to the conative measures.

The overall pattern of distances between clusters shows that the "social distance," "racial traits," "racial violence," "selling a house," and "legislation" clusters are all relatively close.

If we consider the distances between regions, the most isolated cluster for both samples is that of social welfare. Not only is social welfare the most remote cluster, but the correlations between the social welfare responses and the other clusters are either small or negative. For nonideologues the correlations between

Table 6-2

**Correlations Between Social Welfare Responses for Ideologues and Nonideologues**

| Content | Ideologues | | | Nonideologues | | |
|---|---|---|---|---|---|---|
| | Jobs | Care | Schools | Jobs | Care | Schools |
| Government jobs | — | | | — | | |
| Medical care | .20 | — | | .28 | | |
| Black schools | .22 | .14 | — | .19 | .17 | — |

Table 6-3
Average Correlations Within Clusters for Ideologues and Nonideologues

| Cluster | Ideologues | Nonideologues |
|---|---|---|
| Social welfare | .19 | .21 |
| Racial traits | .27 | .31 |
| Civil liberties | .15 | .09 |
| Social distance | .44 | .43 |
| Fair hiring | .42 | .48 |
| Selling house | .70 | .77 |
| Legislation | .19 | .18 |
| Racial violence | .29 | .11 |
| Awareness | .19 | .18 |
| Action | .31 | .28 |

"government jobs" and some action items are, for example: "child play" $-.13$, "marry black" $-.05$, and "open housing" $-.03$. The "social welfare" and "awareness" clusters are the most remote for the ideologue group. "Social welfare" correlates with "unemployment" $-.07$, "housing quality" $-.07$, "teacher quality" $-.07$, "job discrimination" $-.16$, and "housing discrimination" $-.20$. The fact that social welfare responses are situated in the most isolated region of both spaces suggests the separation between attitudes in the social welfare and civil rights arenas, or perhaps more accurately, between economic and noneconomic liberalism.

Most interestingly, the configuration of points undergoes a marked change from one subsample to the other. The distances between "awareness" and the majority of clusters are greater for nonideologues than ideologues. The action responses are ordered in a similar pattern for both groups. However, the distances between "action" and "awareness" clusters are quite different. The correlations between cognition and action are in fact much higher for ideologues than for nonideologues. Table 6-4 presents the correlations between cognition and action for both groups.

For ideologues the pattern is fairly clear; the correlations are without exception in a positive direction, and nearly half the correlations are significant or nearly significant. However, the correlations of action and cognition are nearly as often negative as positive for nonideologues, and where these correlations are positive most often the ideologues show a higher corresponding association.

These differences suggest that the awareness of racial discrimination and the social and economic plight of blacks is more likely to generalize into the action component of attitudes for ideologues than for nonideologues. In short, the psychological distance between cognition and action is less for those respondents who are ideologues.

79

**Table 6-4**
**Correlations Between Cognition and Action for Ideologues (N=177) and Nonideologues (N-317)**

| | Content | Unemployment | Housing Quality | Teacher Quality | Job Discrimination | Job Discrimination |
|---|---|---|---|---|---|---|
| Ideologues (N=177) | Sell to black | .16 | .05 | .05 | .18 | .04 |
| | Neighbor sell | .23 | .08 | .12 | .19 | .16 |
| | Open housing | .20 | .02 | .10 | .23 | .04 |
| | Bussing proposal | .14 | .03 | .14 | .09 | .10 |
| | Child play | .11 | .09 | .34 | .07 | .26 |
| | House party | .11 | .16 | .04 | .10 | .18 |
| | Date black | .12 | .17 | .11 | .12 | .14 |
| | Marry black | .07 | .16 | .21 | .11 | .06 |
| Nonideologues (N=317) | Sell to black | -.19 | -.11 | -.09 | .07 | .01 |
| | Neighbor sell | -.10 | -.06 | -.08 | .10 | -.01 |
| | Open housing | -.04 | .08 | .01 | .12 | .06 |
| | Bussing proposal | .03 | .03 | -.03 | .10 | .12 |
| | Child play | .13 | .05 | .11 | .02 | .19 |
| | House party | .03 | -.04 | .09 | .07 | .02 |
| | Date black | .01 | -.03 | .05 | .08 | .05 |
| | Marry black | -.02 | -.05 | .03 | .15 | .02 |

The importance of such an association between the cognitive and action components of attitudes, if these data are accurate, can hardly be overemphasized. This finding tentatively indicates that for part of the electorate knowledge of social conditions acts as a positive constraint on belief systems, leading to *more favorable* racial attitudes. However, for the majority of the electorate, awareness of the prevalence of racial disadvantages appears to function in an opposite manner, resulting perhaps in negative feelings toward blacks. We know that nonideologues tend to be somewhat less appreciative of the existence of discrimination. Where they are aware, the system does not seem to benefit by an increase in racial tolerance.

This relationship between cognition and action encourages us to return to the earlier distinction made between the stylistic and ideological attributes of the liberalism-conservatism dimension. It will be recalled that in Chapter 1 we mentioned the possibility that a stylistic attribute may serve as a clue to the attitudes of nonideologues. One's relationship to the status quo can be revealed through responses on action items. Although we lack any definitive measures of behavior, we do have statements respondents made about the manner in which they would behave in certain situations relating to interracial contact. Items regarding the awareness of black disadvantages and racial discrimination can be thought to represent part of the content of a belief system.

As one would expect on the basis of the greater sophistication of ideologues, the stylistic or action component of their belief systems is constrained by their awareness, the content of their beliefs. However, for nonideologues the relationships between style and content are not as strong (Table 6-4). Our earlier proposition that the stylistic attribute is an adequate predictor for nonideologues is not borne out.

In sum, we have had only limited success in assessing the relevance of differences in the belief structures of ideologues and nonideologues. In fact, the data do not appear to support the assumption of a liberalism-conservatism dimension for ideologues any more than for nonideologues. Although we do not encounter a balance structure as indicated by a liberalism-conservatism dimension, several clusters were obtained for both groups. Certainly social welfare and civil rights attitudes are psychologically differentiated for both groups. It seems fair to say that the similarities are as striking as the differences.

Yet the social backgrounds of ideologues and nonideologues are certainly distinctive, and there are significant differences on a number of attitude items. The finding that these differences do not seem to generalize to the structure of belief systems is noteworthy. However, a difference was found in the associations between cognition and action which, while perhaps below acceptable standards of significance, appears worth pursuing in the future. Thus we end up offering some promising experimental evidence.

# 7

## An Interpretative Overview

### Introduction

We have suggested in the previous chapters that for a considerable minority of the Detroit electorate, the liberalism-conservatism dimension is politically meaningful. In the perception of members of that electorate who are ideologues, it is apparent that the two major political parties do not represent the range of that dimension (see Figure 1-1). In terms of the distribution of ideologues it appears that both parties could profit electorally by moves in a conservative direction.

If we consider the distribution of ideologues in Figure 2-2, we can more precisely reveal the gains the parties could expect through changes in their own ideological positions.[1] Table 7-1 suggests that the Democratic party can increase turnout within its share of the vote (52 percent of the total) by moving *either* in a more conservative or a more liberal direction. The greatest gains, however, are to be expected with a move to a more conservative position, where the largest share of ideologues are concentrated. Similarly, the Republican party stands to gain by a move in either direction, and again, gains are maximized by a move to a conservative position.

This discussion is based only on those voters whose party choices were logically consistent with their ideologies. We recall from Table 4-3, however, that a considerable proportion of potential Democratic supporters (14 percent of weak Democrats and 40 percent of Independents with leanings toward the Democratic party) felt that they are more conservative than both major parties. These voters who are off the consistent left-right continuum appear to accentuate pulls in a conservative direction on the Democratic party. Some of these voters might be Southern in-migrants and/or supporters of Wallace in 1968. Although Table 7-1 refers to only 140 respondents in the sample who are ideologues, the results are consistent with research on the national electorate which indicates that "there are several times more votes to be gained by leaning toward Wallace than by leaning toward McCarthy" (Converse et al., 1969:29).

This *conservatism* reflected in the distribution of ideologues in Figures 1-1 and 2-2 is reminiscent of the overwhelming conservatism expressed through the responses of the total sample. For example, 75 percent of the total sample are in favor of allowing police to wiretap telephones.

A "law and order" orientation is dominant in many other items. Fully 80 percent of the sample feel that repressive techniques should be used to prevent

**Table 7-1**
**Effects of an Ideological Shift on the Distribution of Support (N=140)**

|  | Current Support | Effect of Liberal Move | Effect of Conservative Move |
|---|---|---|---|
|  |  | Democratic Party (Percent) |  |
| Organization position | 7 | 21 | 24 |
| Alternative positions |  |  |  |
| Strong partisan | 8 | 8 | 11 |
| Weak partisan | 17 | 12 | 6 |
| Independent—leaning | 11 | 8 | 3 |
| Independent—no leaning | 9 | 3 | 8 |
|  | 52 | 52 | 52 |
|  |  | Republican Party (Percent) |  |
| Organization position | 8 | 16 | 25 |
| Alternative positions |  |  |  |
| Strong partisan | 13 | 14 | 9 |
| Weak partisan | 17 | 10 | 9 |
| Independent—leaning | 6 | 6 | 5 |
| Independent—no leaning | 6 | 4 | 2 |
|  | 50 | 50 | 50 |

Note: The 2 percent Independent floating vote has been included in each column. Total is 52 + 50 − 2 = 100%.

further rioting. A majority (53 percent) rank high on the "F" index, giving conservative responses on all four items. Over 90 percent respond in favor of the city's having a law which would prevent a property owner from keeping junk in his back yard. Relatedly, some 61 percent believe that there should be a law requiring a home owner to keep his grass cut to a reasonable level.

A general conservatism is also apparent in regard to civil rights issues. More than half (59 percent) of the respondents would not sell their house to a black. Moreover, an impressive 89 percent of respondents think their neighbors would not want them to sell to a black customer. And yet, a majority of the total sample feels that it is black inadequacies which account for their disadvantaged position. Fifty-four percent of the sample feel that blacks themselves are responsible for their plight, while one-third (32 percent) place the blame on whites. Some 14 percent give answers which indicate that both black inadequacies and racial discrimination underlie their disadvantages.

Thus, the overall picture is one of conservatism, both in the responses of the total sample, and in the distribution of ideologues along the liberalism-conservatism dimension. It will be recalled that many of the differences found between the attitudes of ideologues and nonideologues were minimal.

## Values and Political Belief Systems

The high degree of uniformity in responses among our respondents suggests that there are similar motivational bases underlying their attitudes. As the source of this uniformity we propose that *values are the most central components* in a belief system. All attitudes can be seen as expressive of certain values.[2] If one is to treat the complex sources of constraint among political beliefs we feel that consideration must be given to the motivational impact of values. Campbell et al. (1960) conclude "that the typical American lacks a clearly patterned ideology of such breadth" (1960:197). However, as mentioned in Chapter 1, the political beliefs of nonideologues may be seen as involving the pursuit of "expressive goals," and in this way their beliefs are organized. Values then *underlie* belief systems.

While few scholars emphasize this approach, we find many suggesting its merit. "The conception of personality as referring to certain characteristic lines of organization from deeper dynamics to surface behavior is often useful" (Campbell et al., 1960:502).

We now turn to a discussion of the cultural level in order to trace the impact of values on political beliefs. In American history both *freedom* and *equality* have occupied central roles. Hartz (1955:89) speaks of "two national impulses bound to make themselves felt: the impulse toward democracy and the impulse toward capitalism," each involving a central value, freedom and equality respectively. Lane writes of freedom and equality as "democracy's two greatest ideals" (1962:81). Rokeach (1969b:169) sees freedom and equality as *the* distinct political value. In fact, Rokeach (1973) feels that freedom and equality represent a two-dimensional model for describing all the major variations among political groupings.

However, out of the liberal tradition one value appears to have arisen as superordinate—freedom. We are, Hartz feels, a Lockean society characterized by our preoccupation with freedom. The master assumption of American political thought is the reality of atomistic social freedom. Lane (1962:349-350) speaks of the "almost universal acceptance of the same Lockean model." Rokeach (1969b) has found freedom to be uniformly ranked high by groups of various political orientations. Relatedly, Boorstin (1953) suggests that the "genius of American politics," lies precisely in this uniformity. His concept of "giveness" refers to the supposedly universal notion that values are implicit in the American experience. Political orthodoxy is so pervasive that the label "unAmerican" is immediately suggestive of subversion. Yet, "Who would think of using the word 'unItalian' or 'unFrench' as we use the word 'unAmerican'?" (Boorstin, 1953:14).

Hugo Munsterburg wrote, near the turn of the century, about the ambivalence even the American laborer felt toward equality:

The American labourer does not feel that his position is inferior; he knows that he has an equal opportunity with everybody else, and the idea of entire equality does not attract him, and would even deprive him of what he holds most valuable—namely, his self-initiative, which aims for the highest social reward as recognition of the highest individual achievement (1904:323).

The orientation toward achievement which grew up with the country continues to place the responsibility for one's status squarely on the shoulders of the individual (Lane, 1962).[3]

The dominance of Lockeanism in our political theory has had tremendous consequences. Hartz (1955), Boorstin (1953), and other commentators have explained how conflicts within a liberal tradition assume a limited range. The total spectrum of political variation does not exist in American politics (Rokeach, 1973).

The keynote of the American political system is said by these commentators to be the inarticulate character of our political theory resulting from the remarkable agreement on social values.[4]

One consequence of this latency is that the American finds it difficult to argue about political principles, and there is little doubt that one reason why Americans become so furious over the arguments of the Communists is that their own political principles are hard to tear from their native bed in the unconscious (Lane, 1962:349-350).

The *uniformity* among the mass public is paralleled by a lack of ideological cleavage between the major parties.

The small ideological difference between our two political parties may be accounted for by the fact that their only disagreement is over means. Both Democrats and Republicans have, on the whole, the same vision of the kind of society there ought to be in the United States (Boorstin, 1953:137).

The ideological similarity of the two major American political parties is surely more often noted than are any differences between them. Campbell and Valen (1964), for example, on the basis of a comparative study of the United States and Norway, point out that 40 percent of their American sample thought that the two major parties were about the same, and an additional 8 percent of the sample did not know if there were differences between the parties. The corresponding figures for the Norwegian sample were 11 percent and 8 percent.

In discussing the foundations of political consciousness we must consider what assumptions the electorate holds. Virtually all voters today, it seems, assume the political desirability of freedom.[5] As Hess and Torney (1968:8) explain, the values of society are "transmitted through child-rearing and other teaching practices to children who, when they become adults, reinforce and help to maintain the culture in which they live." The appeals of the major parties to the electorate rely on this value consensus.

Where most citizens differ is in the degree of their commitment to equality. That this is a valid description of persons is indicated by the experimental evidence of Rokeach (1969b). He found very significant differences in the centrality of the value of equality among political orientations. Freedom was ranked high by all major political groupings in American society, whereas there was variation in equality. This suggests that it is the *distance* between the two values that is crucial. The question then becomes not which value is most important, but by how much does freedom overshadow equality.[6] More effectively than any other value, equality differentiates positions along the political spectrum. The political spectrum in the United States, Rokeach (1973) submits, is really an *equality dimension*.

The consensus on the value of freedom can be seen as underlying the uniformity in political beliefs. But more than this, the differences that are apparent in the beliefs of ideologues and nonideologues can be explained in part by variation in the centrality of equality. There are a number of items that can be used in a consideration of equality. Let us take the question on civil disorders. If in fact there is a significant distance between freedom and equality in a respondent's belief system, this imbalance could "translate" itself into a concern for crime and lawlessness. Those who rank equality lower should be likely to recommend repressive solutions for racial disturbances. By this reasoning we would conclude that since ideologues are significantly less likely to express a repressive solution, for them equality is more central.

Why are ideologues somewhat more concerned about equality than non-ideologues, as indicated by their more favorable attitudes on the majority of civil rights issues? Perhaps part of the answer lies in the association between education and the value of equality. As a group, ideologues are considerably more educated than nonideologues. Education appears to underlie less simplistic ways of perceiving social problems. Just as a college education provides the constraints necessary to a "full-blown ideology," it may sensitize the recipient to the value of equality, lessening the distance in one's value hierarchy between freedom and equality. For some perhaps a concern for equality could result from socialization into the world of academics who hold the value of equality (Lipset, 1963).

The effects of higher education, though, may be more a function of change in social position. Education improves one's status and helps to provide a more secure social position. In this sense the impact of education on one's racial attitudes is an indirect consideration. A person who is highly educated may not need to be as preoccupied with his own well being; he can, based on his higher status position, "afford" a greater concern for equality. That equality may be perceived by ideologues as less of a threat than by nonideologues is suggested by the finding that nonideologues are more fearful of violence by blacks (Tables 3-4 and 3-5). The value of equality is certainly more in harmony with support for civil rights issues than is a preoccupation with freedom.

To evaluate the significance of education we cross-tabulated each of the background factors against racial attitudes and found that consistent and sharp differences occurred only with variation by education and age. Of these two factors, education is the most important. To illustrate this, in Table 7-2 we present attitudes which are significantly differentiated by education. The most obvious difference is that on every attitude item the more educated respondents give the more liberal responses.

Education is also not surprisingly a definite factor in the solution respondents

**Table 7-2**
**Racial Attitudes by Education**

| Content | Educational Level | |
|---|---|---|
| | Less than College | Some College + |
| | (Percent) | |
| Whites should organize against black violence | 31 | 17 |
| Unemployment is a lot greater among blacks | 34 | 59 |
| Some danger of black violence | 68 | 51 |
| Housing discrimination is a lot greater among blacks | 38 | 69 |
| Employment discrimination is a lot greater among blacks | 10 | 19 |
| Respondent gets together socially with blacks | 18 | 33 |

Note: Of the 639 respondents for whom we have data on education, there are 455 with less than, and 184 with more than, some college education. The Ns vary across each attitude item but there is never a total base for the attitudes of less than 592 cases. Accordingly, there are never fewer than 420 respondents with less than some college education and 172 respondents with some college.

recommend regarding riot prevention. The relationship is *linear*. Only one in ten of those with less than a high school education mention improving the conditions behind the riot, whereas almost half (47 percent) of respondents with at least a college education apparently see the primacy of treating causes over punishing black rioters.

## Ideology, Values, and the American Party System

One can understand the tendency of the major parties to down play ideological cleavages in terms of the discussion on values. Political parties do not exist merely to accumulate as many votes as possible. The different theories of Downs (1957) and Riker (1967) illustrate this debate. While Downs contends that parties attempt to maximize electoral support, Riker amends this approach suggesting a "minimax" strategy is more typical of the parties. For our purposes we could say that party officials, and office holders who were elected on the party ticket, hold certain issue positions which, in the aggregate, make up the position of the party. In seeking support for the party, these officials appear to adopt a minimax decision rule. That is, where necessary to gain the support they need to translate party positions into public policy, they will modify their positions. Once they have the necessary support, however, their commitment to their issue positions prevents them from further altering these positions in order to further increase their support.

We suggest that a major party is going to seek new supporters *only* if the party leaders are reasonably certain that they are in a position to maintain the present distribution of power in spite of the recruitment of new persons. The degree to which the parties do not attempt to recruit outside forces is striking.[7] The number of political activists is known to be functionally related to the behavior of the party (Eldersveld, 1963).

Considering alternative models of political involvement, Eldersveld (1963:454) feels that his data most readily support the theory that sees party contact as leading to public awareness about politics, rather than the theory which sees the parties as seeking out the political activist. For the minority of the mass public exposed to the party organization "the party effort is clearly functional to political interest, involvement, and consensual support of the political system" (Eldersveld, 1963:523). Similarly, Katz and Eldersveld (1961) tested the impact of party activity upon the electorate, and found that for the Republican party in Detroit, the strength of party leadership was a significant variable in "voting behavior."

That the values of the more politically involved are in part responsible for the structuring of mass belief systems is suggested by the findings of Alford and Scoble (1968). They argue, "the fact that high-status, home-owning, organizationally-active persons provide half of all highly involved persons suggests that politics in American cities is probably disproportionately influenced by the norms and values characteristic of that group—if it is a group with distinctive norms and values" (Alford and Scoble, 1968:1206). Relatedly, Eldersveld (1963:432) notes how not only are personal drives dominant in party politics, but these drives are reinforced by the system. "The ordinary activist sees the party as *motivationally* satisfying and instrumental" (Eldersveld, 1963:530). (Italics mine.)

This evidence suggests that party activists are concerned about the maximization of electoral strength only within the constraints of their personal values. Thus the political information, including ideological appeals, to which voters attend can be seen as limited in two directions. First of all it is limited by the volume of output of the party system, and second, it is limited by the voter's motivation to receive political communications, once some flow exists (Converse, 1962:586).

As Campbell et al. point out, awareness is "partly a matter of motivation and predisposition: the individual is aware of things he wants to attend" (Campbell et al., 1960:60). Moreover, the "decisions of those who control communication" are also "partial determinants of public awareness . . ." (Campbell et al., 1960:60). The American political system places a heavy burden upon its citizens for their own political education. While our society has the largest proportion of college graduates in the world (Merelman, 1969:751), political activism is only typical of a small minority of the electorate.

The major parties do not function so as to appeal to the electorate in clear-cut ideological appeals. McClosky, (1960:420) notes that ". . . the American parties make only a feeble effort to educate the rank and file politically, and since no central source exists for the authoritative pronouncement of party policy, the followers often do not know what their leaders believe or on what issues the parties chiefly divide." "The followers, in short, are less often and less effectively indoctrinated than their leaders" (McClosky, 1960:421).

The reluctance of the major parties to put forward clear-cut ideological appeals is reflected in our finding that there are positions on the liberalism-conservatism dimension that do not seem to be represented by the party system (see Figure 1-1).[8] To focus our attention exclusively on those voters to whom the major parties appeal may mean that we overlook certain segments of the electorate.

The data on organizational partisans bear out the muting of ideological appeals. Respondents who occupy an ideological position congruent with that of one of the major parties tend to be strong partisans (Table 2-7). Moreover, these respondents appear to hold views that would make them attractive to the parties. On the other hand, persons who occupy positions beyond the major parties are less likely to be strong partisans, and their attitudes might make them less attractive to the parties.

There is some justification for concluding that liberals and conservatives occupy the positions they do as a result of the major parties' reluctance to appeal to them. There is also a *contradiction* between this kind of political calculus and the functioning of democracy as a political process. Perhaps the primary function of politics and government is conflict resolution. The democratic process may be seen as one of collective bargaining, in which a series of interests are represented in an institutional arena that can make value-allocative decisions. The various interests, in turn, regard these decisions as binding because they have a means of making their claims within the political structure.

The chief, though certainly not the only, linkage between these interests and the government is the political parties, which themselves must reconcile demands of several interests that at times are incompatible with each other. Where the range of interests is not represented by the parties (and this would seem to be the case in Detroit), these interests may seek alternate channels into the democratic process, or perhaps not vote at all. Thus the political parties, in their tendencies to seek satisfactory rather than maximal support, may fail to represent the range of political ideas, and promote behavior dysfunctional for the system.

Summing up, we feel that one weakness of the present theory on belief systems is a lack of understanding of the factors which constrain political beliefs. While we have not been able to directly assess the motivational impact of values on belief systems, some of the evidence regarding civil rights attitudes indicates the centrality of the value of freedom in the belief systems of our respondents.

It may be useful to consider the uniformity in values when explaining the often minimal differences in attitudes between ideologues and nonideologues. At the same time, the attitude differences that are apparent can perhaps be related to the variation in the concern for social equality.

## Stability of the American Political System

In contrast to the position taken by Berelson et al. (1954) that uninvolved voters are functional for the political system, Converse and Dupeux (1962) have suggested that a widespread and deep-rooted sense of partisan identification in the electorate has been responsible, in large measure, for the relative stability of the American political system, and that conversely, the large proportion of voters without party identification in the French electorate was in part responsible for the instability of the French party system. Converse (1969) has also suggested that as a party system reaches maturity, within about three generations, the level of party identification in its electorate reaches an equilibrium point of about 72 percent.

Inglehart and Hochstein (1972) have noted that party identification in the

United States has dropped below the equilibrium point of Converse's model, and suggest that the process, which they anticipate will involve even lower rates of partisanship in the future, is one of *dealignment*—declining rates of identification with any party—rather than realignment. The most dramatic manifestation of the dealignment is the increased proportion of the electorate considering itself to be Independent at all ages.

Our own data on Independents, on strength of partisanship, and on the ideological positions of partisans vis-à-vis their parties lead us to accept the dealignment hypothesis. Despite differences between our Detroit sample and the national electorate, we feel that our data reflect national trends. At the same time, we stress that this dealignment implies neither depoliticization nor deideologization of the electorate. Unlike the portrayal of the apathetic independent of the 1950s, we see the Independent and the weak partisan of the 1970s as an aware, informed, concerned voter who is dissatisfied with the alternatives furnished to him by the Democratic and Republican parties. Moreover, rather than seeing changes in the political independent and in the ideological distance between the partisan and his party as isolated phenomena, we view them as manifestations, albeit extreme ones, of more sweeping changes in the American electorate at large. We see indications both of a general dissatisfaction with the current major parties and, more specifically, of a wider range of ideological positions than the parties represent. To the extent that the parties are responsive to voter demands, we would anticipate either the development of greater ideological differences between the major parties or the increased incidence of minor parties (particularly at the local level) which, while they are unlikely to come to dominate the electoral arena, might well have a major impact on the nature of American politics.

We have considered certain correlates of political ideology—social background, attitudes, and personality characteristics. These analyses, particularly with regard to the deviant categories of the organizational partisans and the marked variability among the subgroup of Independent ideologues, suggest that we would do well to move beyond the simplified conception of our political system inherent in the conventional unidimensional approach to the patterning of beliefs.

# Appendixes

# Appendix A:
## Cover Sheet and
## Interview Schedule

University of Michigan                                        Cover Sheet
Detroit Area Study
Project 981
April, 1969

Final interviewer's name to be entered here by interviewer

                                                    Your Interview No.

Sample Address:

Street No.        Street            Apt. No.       Segment No.    Block No.
                                                   and Line

City or Town                  Tract No.

A. Are there any *other* dwelling units at the sample address that are *not* already
   listed on the segment listing sheet?

   1. Yes          5. No   Go to C

B. Unlisted Dwelling Form
   Record all unlisted dwelling units found from step A above. If there are 3 or
   fewer listings *make cover sheets* for each and interview there. If there are
   more than 3 listings, contact supervisor. Return new cover sheets along with
   this one.

   Suffix to          Street number        For DU's discovered by step
   be added to        and name             A, indicate location within
   sample no.                              sample address structure.
     -a
     -b
     -c

C. Hello, I'm                from the University of Michigan. We are doing an
   interview survey in the Detroit area. You should have received a letter from
   the University saying I would call. [Explain as necessary: chance sampling;
*Note: Throughout this Appendix the word "Negro" has been changed to "black."

93

confidentiality (statistical only); sponsorship (U. of M.); and purpose. Show your copy of letter]

In order to know who to interview, I need to know who the head of the house is? Unless R says "my husband" ask: Are you (is he or she) single, married, divorced, widowed, or separated? Enter proper information on head and wife (if any) below and make proper selection. If head has no spouse, cross out box 2 under head: if spouse, write "wife". (See manual for age restriction.)

a. Relation    b. Sex    c. Race       d. Age    e. Marital      Check (√)
   to head                (Observe)               Status          Respondent
1. Head
2.

Selection of Respondent:
If DU includes *only* head, take head
If DU includes *both* head and wife take:
    Head        Head's
                Wife

D. Description of dwelling unit address: must be filled out on first visit to segment, i.e., *before* contacting anyone at D.U.

   300.  Description of the house.
         1. Single family dwelling
         2. Flat in two or three family dwelling
         3. Flat in apartment building
              Total number of dwelling units in this building    Approx.
         7. Other (specify)

   301.  Estimate R's yearly family income from *external* appearance of house and property (do *not* later adjust for income from interview.)
         1. Low income (less than $5,000)
         2. Low medium ($5,000 to $8,000)
         3. Medium (8,000 to $11,000)
         4. High medium ($11,000 to $16,000)
         5. High ($16,000 and over)

   302.  External condition of the house
         1. Excellent; expensive house, well cared for.
         2. Average house; good repair, well kept up.
         3. Average house; not good repair.
         4. Poor; ramshackle, much in need of repair.

303. How does R's house compare in general appearance with the half-dozen houses nearest to it?
    1. Respondent's house is above average, relative to the others.
    2. Respondent's house is average.
    3. Respondent's house is below average relative to the others.

304. Are there private homes surrounding the house on both sides and across the street, *or* are there any apartment houses, commercial establishments, etc.
    1. *Only* private homes
    7. Other (*specify clearly*)

305. Is R's house on the *corner* of the block?
    1. Yes
    5. No

306. Is the street the house faces on a regular residential street, or is it three or more lanes wide or a busy street?
    1. Regular residential street
    7. Other (describe)

307. Distance of R's house (structure, not yard) from nearest house on each side (measured in average car lengths). Check left & right.

                                              House to Left          House to Right
    1. *One* car length or less
    2. *One* to *two* car lengths
    3. *Two* to *three* car lengths
    4. *Three* to *four* car lengths
    5. More than *four* car lengths
        (e.g., vacant lot)

308. Relation of R's house *yard* to yards of other houses.
    1. Sharply separated on *both* sides by high bushes, fences, or other barriers.
    2. Separated on one or both sides but not so clearly. (e.g., driveways, low or scattered shrubbery, other minor divisions.)
    3. Lack of separation between yards.
    7. Other (*specify*)

309. How closed are the shades, curtains, or drapes in the main front rooms of R's DU?
    1. Completely or almost completely closed.
    2. Partly closed (or some open and some closed)
    3. Quite open

310. Within a block of the segment is there a park or other common area where children or adults can gather for recreational or social purposes?
    1. Yes
    2. No

311. Indicate any other ways in which the house or immediate neighborhood is unusual (e.g., garden apartments, town house, row houses, etc.):

E. Call Record
   Call Number                          1  2  3  4  5  6  More (specify)
   1.    Hour of day
         (include am/pm)
   2.    Date
   3.    Day of week
   4.    Interv. *name*
   5.    Result of call
         (use abbrev. from G)

F. Space for comments on noninterviews: give date and your name for each comment. (For refusals, indicate whether R knew anything about racial aspect of interview and if it affected refusal.)
   Date        Interviewer

G. Final Outcome
   Check *one* after *final* disposition of cover sheet. For intermediate calls enter appropriate abbreviation in F.
   ☐ 1. *INT* :    Interview completed     ☐ 5. *NAH* :  No one at home
                   successfully                          (after required
                                                         callbacks)
   ☐ 2. *HV* :     House vacant            ☐ 6. *RA* :   Respondent himself
                                                         himself absent
                                                         (after required
                                                         callback)
   ☐ 3. *NER* :    No eligible             ☐ 7. *REF* :  Refusal. (describe
                   respondent in                         fully under F.)
                   DU (specify             ☐ 8. *Other* : (describe
                   under F.)                             clearly under F.)
   ☐ 4. *Not DU* : Address not
                   a dwelling.
                   (explain
                   under F.)

Interviewer
Interview No.
Segment No.

## The Detroit Metropolitan Area Survey

*Time started:
1. Were you born and raised in the Detroit area?
    1. Yes (go to Q.2)          5. No. ( *Ask A, B, & C* )
    A. How long have you lived in the Detroit area?     years.
    B. In what state did you live *longest* when you were a child?
    [state (or country if not U.S.A.)]
    C. Was that in a large city (over 100,000 people), a small city,
    a small town, or on a farm?
                                   1. Large city
                                   2. Small city
                                   3. Small town
                                   4. Farm

2. What in your opinion are the two or three main problems facing people in
   areas like the Greater Detroit area? [If only *one* given, probe for second: "Is
   there any other problem you would like to mention?]

3. (Thinking of the national scene) who are the one or two national leaders that
   you admire most in the United States today?

(Here are several issues that have been in the news recently. Would you please
give your opinion on each.)

4. Do you think the federal government should in some way provide jobs for
   people who are unemployed and can't find work?
                                   1. Yes
                                   2. Yes, but volunteers
                                      qualification (*specify*)
                                   3. No

*5. Some neighborhoods have schools with rundown buildings and less-trained
    teachers than other neighborhoods. Do you think the federal government
    should provide more money to bring the poor schools up to the standard of
    the better schools, or that the government shouldn't do this?

1. Should provide money
2. Should provide but
   volunteers qualification
   (*specify*)
3. Should *not* provide

6. Do you think the federal government should guarantee free medical and hospital care for everyone?

    1. Yes
    2. Yes, but volunteers
       qualification (*specify*)
    3. No

7. Do you think the police should be allowed to wiretap telephones and listen in on private conversations when they think it is necessary for collecting evidence to solve crimes?

    1. Yes
    5. No

8. In the past few years some movies have come out in which actors appear with little or no clothes on. Do you think such movies should be *banned* for everyone, or that adults have a right to see whatever they want.

    1. Should be banned
    2. Adults have right to
      see what they want

9. There are a few people in this country who consider themselves Communists. Do you think Communists living here in the United States are now a very great danger, a great danger, some danger, or hardly any danger?

    1. A very great danger
    2. A great danger
    3. Some danger
    4. Hardly any danger

Now I'd like to ask you a few questions about your immediate neighborhood—that is, the five or six (houses/apartments) nearest to yours.

10. First, how many years have you lived on this block?

    years [if less than one year, give in months]

11. [No question]

12. Thinking of the five or six neighbors nearest your (house/apartment), which of the following best describes the relations you personally have with most of these neighbors. Here are four possibilities. [show card and read]

   1. Often visit in one another's homes.
   2. Frequently chat in the yard or on the sidewalk.
   3. Occasionally chat in the yard or on the sidewalk.
   4. Hardly know the neighbors.
   5. Volunteers that it is different for different neighbors
      (probe and record so that office coding of "most neighbors"
      will be possible).

13. [If married, ask:]
How about your (wife/husband): Which of those possibilities best describes the relations your (wife/husband) has with your five or six nearest neighbors. [show card and read again]
   1. Often visit in one another's homes.
   2. Frequently chat in the yard or on the sidewalk.
   3. Occasionally chat in the yard or on the sidewalk.
   4. Hardly know the neighbors.
   5. Volunteers that it is different for different neighbors
      (probe and record so that office coding of "most neighbors"
      will be possible).

14. Are there any ways in which you and your near neighbors do favors for each other, such as loaning things, watching children, or something else?
   Yes (ask A)                  4. No

   A. Is this at least once or twice a week, once or twice a month,
      or only a few times a year?
                    0. Inapplicable
                    1. Once or twice a week
                    2. Once or twice a month
                    3. Few times a year

15. Of your best friends and close relatives, do any live in the five or six (houses/apartments) nearest to yours?

   1. Yes (ask A)              5. No (ask B)
     A. Is this mainly one          B. Do you have close
        family, two families,           friends or relatives
        or more than two?             living within a block
                              or two of here?

1. One family      1. Yes
2. Two      5. No
3. More than two

16. Suppose you were going to remodel and paint the outside of your house, and you found out that several of your neighbors felt the change would spoil the looks of the neighborhood. Would you try to work something out that was more satisfactory to them, or would you go ahead the way you had already planned?

     1. Would try to work something out to satisfy neighbors
     2. Go ahead as planned

*17. Suppose you heard the house next door was being sold. Which one of the following characteristics would you most hope the family moving in would have [show card, read alternatives, and check 1st choice].

     A. Which characteristic would you next prefer in a family moving next door? (Check second choice.)

|  | 17. First Choice | A. Second Choice |
|---|---|---|
| 1. College graduate | | |
| 2. Quiet and agreeable | | |
| 3. Is a leader in solving neighborhood problems | | |
| 4. Has well-behaved children | | |
| 5. Friendly and outgoing | | |
| 6. Keep up their house and yard | | |

18. All in all, how satisfied are you with living in this neighborhood: are you very satisfied, fairly satisfied, somewhat dissatisfied, or very dissatisfied?

1. Very      2. Fairly      3. Somewhat
Satisfied      Satisfied      Dissatisfied

4. Very Dissatisfied

19. Do you plan to move out of this neighborhood in the next 2 or 3 years?
     1. Yes (ask A)      5. No
     A. Why do you plan to move?

20. Cities have some laws about what home owners can do with heir property. Do you think the city should prevent a property owner from keeping junk in

his back yard, even if it isn't dangerous?

1. Yes
5. No

21. How about a law requiring a home owner to keep his grass cut to a reasonable level. Do you think there should be such a law or not?

1. Should be a law
5. Not a law

22. Now I'm going to read a number of statements to you that some people agree with and some people disagree with. For each one, would you say whether you mostly agree with it or mostly disagree with it?

[If R ever hesitates, say: You need not agree or disagree completely, just indicate whether you *tend* more to agree or to disagree with it.]

Here's the first:                                    Agree          Disagree

A. Obedience and respect for authority are the most important virtues children should learn.

B. The raising of one's social position is one of the more important goals in life.

C. It is important for friends to have about the same opinions on things.

D. High schools should *not* try to set rules on the length of a boy's hair.

E. To compromise with one's enemies is dangerous because it usually leads to betrayal of one's own side.

F. The police need more freedom to crack down on criminals.

G. One should always try to live in a highly respectable community even if it means sacrificing other things.

H. Young people sometimes get rebellious ideas, but as they grow up they ought to get over them and settle down.

I. A person should fit his own ideas and behavior to the group that he is with at the time.

J. Most people can be trusted.

Agree          Disagree

K. There are two kinds of people in the world, those who are for truth and those who are against truth.

L. No decent, normal person would ever think of hurting a close friend or relative.

M. It is best to go one's own way regardless of the opinions of others.

N. Although we should try to sympathize with mental patients, we cannot expect to understand their odd behavior.

O. Teenage boys who insist on wearing long hair should *not* be allowed in regular schools.

P. Most people will take advantage of another person if given a chance.

Q. Most of our social problems could be solved if we could somehow get rid of the immoral and crooked people.

23. Suppose in a restaurant a waitress spills a full bowl of soup on a customer's dress. The customer is upset and complains loudly about the clumsiness of the waitress. If you were in the restaurant and saw this, would you have any particular feelings toward the waitress or the customer?

    A. If answer was "none", ask: Would you have any feelings at all about the situation? If answer was unclear, ask: Would you have any other feelings?

Here are some questions on racial matters in Detroit. The first few are more factual, and we would like you just to give your best idea about them, even though you may not be completely sure.

24. First, we'd like to get your idea of the number of white and black people in the city of Detroit—*not* the suburbs but *just the city*. Would you say blacks make up less than a quarter of the city population, between a quarter and a half, about half, or more than half the population?

         1. Less than quarter
         2. Quarter to half
         3. About half
         4. More than half

25. Now, considering *both* city *and* suburbs together, would you say that the black population in the general Detroit area is growing faster than the white population, at about the same speed, or slower than the white population?
    Black faster (*ask A*)     3. Same          4. Black slower

    A. Do you think it's growing just a little faster or a lot faster?
       1. Little faster                      2. Lot faster

26. The rest of these questions also refer to the *Greater* Detroit area—that is, *both the city and suburbs combined*. [If R ever asks, remind him that Detroit refers to city and surrounding suburbs combined.]

    Do you think unemployment in the Detroit area is greater among blacks, greater among whites, or about the same for both?

    Greater among *blacks*          3. Same          4. Greater among *whites*
    (*ask A*)

    A. Do you think there is a lot more unemployment among blacks or just a little more?
       1. Lot                    2. Little

27. How about the quality of housing that white people and blacks have: Is the housing worse for the average black family, worse for the average white family, or is there not much difference?
    Black worse (*ask A*)       3. Not much difference     4. White worse

    A. Do you think black housing is just a little worse or a lot worse?
       1. Little worse           2. Lot worse

28. Do you think the quality of teachers and schools in black areas of Detroit is better than in white areas, about the same, or worse?
       1. Black better           2. Same                3. Black worse

29. Where blacks *are* behind whites in such things as jobs or income or housing, do you think this is mainly due to something about blacks themselves, or mainly due to the way whites have treated blacks in the past?
       1. Something about blacks   2. Way whites have    3. Other (*specify*)
          (*ask A and B*)             (*ask C*)             fully what R
                                                            means)

       A. What is it about blacks      C. Would you explain
          that makes them have            what you have in
          worse jobs, income, or          mind?
          housing?

30. There's a lot of talk about poverty and poor people these days. Of the people in Detroit who are poor, would you say most are white, most are black, or are there about the same number of each?

    1. Most *white*          2. About same          3. Most *black*

31. How about crimes such as robbery and assault in the Detroit area—would you say almost all such crimes are committed by blacks, more than half by blacks, about half, or less than half?

    1. Almost all by blacks
    2. More than half
    3. About half
    4. Less than half

32. Do you think the victims of black crimes are mostly black or mostly white?

    1. Mostly black
    2. Mostly white
    3. Half and half
    [if volunteered]

33. How much danger, if any, do you think there is of groups of blacks from the inner city going out to the white areas and suburbs to commit violence on whites: Do you think this is a great danger, some danger, little danger, or no danger?

    1. Great danger
    2. Some danger
    3. Little danger
    4. No danger

34. Some people want to organize whites into groups to protect themselves against violence by blacks. Do you think this is a good idea or not?

    1. Good idea
    2. Not a good idea

35. What do you think is the most important thing the city government in Detroit could do to keep a riot like the one in 1967 from breaking out again?

36. All in all, would you guess that most blacks in Detroit are pretty content with the way things are, or would you say most are discontent?

    1. Most content
    2. Most discontent

A. What sort of blacks would you say are *most* discontent? (be sure to probe unclear responses).

37. Do you think most blacks would rather live in mixed black-white neighborhoods or in separate all-black neighborhoods?
    1. Mixed black-white
    2. Separate all-black

38. Suppose you knew that a person's ancestry was mainly white but also part black. From his appearance, however, people would think that he was all white. Would you consider such a person white or black?
    1. White
    2. Black
    3. Mulatto (*volunteered*)
    4. Would consider him as an individual (*volunteered*)
    5. Would consider him whatever he considered himself (*volunteered*)

39. (Turning to another matter on race.) Have you personally ever had any difficulty getting a job or advancing in a job because blacks were being given the advantage over whites?
    1. Yes (*ask A and C*)        5. No (*ask B and C*)

A. What was it that happened?    B. Has it happened to anyone you know personally?
                                       1. Yes (*ask C*)
                                       5. No (*ask C*)

Ask everyone
C. Do you think it happens fairly often in the Detroit area?
    1. Yes
    5. No

40. Some people in the Detroit area have felt they had to move from a neighborhood because blacks were moving in and it was causing problems for their family. Have you ever moved from a neighborhood partly for this reason?
    1. Yes                        5. No (*ask A*)
                              A. Has anyone you know personally moved partly for this reason?
                                       1. Yes
                                       5. No

41. If two or three black families move into a white neighborhood do you see any sorts of problems as likely to arise?
    1. Yes (*ask A*)          5. No
    A. What sorts of problems are likely to arise?

42. (If property value decline *not* mentioned to Q. 41): When two or three black families move into a white neighborhood, do you think property values always go down, usually go down, only sometimes go down, or don't go down at all?
    1. Always
    2. Usually
    3. Sometimes
    4. Don't go down at all

43. Would you say there's a lot of discrimination against blacks when they look for a job in the Detroit area or little discrimination?
    1. Lot
    2. Little
    3. None at all (*volunteered*)

44. How about in buying or renting a home in the Detroit area: would you say there's a lot of discrimination against blacks trying to get a home or little discrimination?
    1. Lot
    2. Little
    3. None at all (*volunteered*)

45. Here are some characteristics sometimes mentioned about people. For each one, would you tell me whether you think it is more true of whites, about equally true of blacks and whites, or more true of blacks?

    The first is "being good in sports." *Regardless of how differences come about*, do you think that "being good in sports" is more true of whites, more true of blacks, or equally true of blacks and whites? [repeat same form for B & C, including "Regardless of how differences come about, do you think. . . ." Repeat later as necessary in asking D, E, F.]

|  | 1. More true of whites | 2. About equal | 3. More true of blacks |
|---|---|---|---|
| A) Being good in sports | | | |
| B) Being inclined toward violence | | | |
| C) Having high ambition | | | |

D)  Having high morals
E)  Being stubborn
F)  Taking care of one's family

G)  [If R said "being good in sports" is more true of blacks, ask:]
    (Going back for a moment,) you said you thought "being good in sports" is more true of blacks than of whites. Do you think blacks are just *naturally* better at sports, or that it's something about the way they are brought up? (*accept DK without probing*)

    1. Naturally
    2. Way brought up
    8. Don't know (*volunteered*)

H)  [If R said "having high ambition" is more true of whites, ask:]
    (Going back a moment,) you said you thought "having high ambition" is more true of whites than of blacks. Do you think whites are just naturally more ambitious, or that it's something about the way they are brought up? (*accept DK without probing*)

    1. Naturally
    2. Way brought up
    8. Don't know (*volunteered*)

I)  [If R said "Being inclined toward violence" is more true of blacks, ask:]
    (Going back for a moment,) you said you thought "being inclined toward violence" is more true of blacks than of whites. Do you think blacks are just naturally more inclined toward violence, or that it's something about the way they are brought up? (*accept DK without probing*)

    1. Naturally
    2. Way brought up
    8. Don't know (*volunteered*)

J)  In general, do you think blacks are as intelligent as white people—that is, can they learn just as well if they are given the same education? (*accept DK without probing*)

    1. Yes
    5. No
    8. Don't know (*volunteered*)

46. Here are some situations where you might have to decide on a particular action. Suppose you owned a house on this block and you wanted to sell it. If a black couple who could afford it wanted to buy it, would you sell to them *if you had a choice*?

    1. Yes (*ask B, D*)                    2. Yes, with qualification
                                              (*record and ask B and D*)

5. No (*ask B, E*)

6. Must sell because of law
(*ask A*)
A. What if there were no law, would
you sell if you had a choice?
1. Yes (*ask B, D*)
5. No (*ask B, E*)

*Ask everyone*

B. Thinking of your five or six closest neighbors here, what do you think
they would want you to do if they knew you had a black customer for
your house? Would they want you to sell to the black or not to sell?
1. Sell it
2. Don't sell
3. Neighbors disagree among
selves (*volunteered*)
(*specify*)
4. They wouldn't care
(*volunteered*) (*ask C*)

C. What do you think most of your
neighbors right around here would
do if they were in the same situation?
1. Sell
2. Not sell

[*NB. everyone is asked either D or E*]
[*If yes to Q. 46 or 46A.*]
D. Suppose the situation
were more complicated.
Several nearby neighbors
come to you and urge you
not to sell to blacks,
because they are worried
about what it will do to
the neighborhood and to
their homes. Would you
sell to the black couple
in this situation if you
had a choice?
1. Yes
5. No

[*If no to Q. 46 or 46A.*]
E. Suppose the situation
were more complicated.
The black buyer in this
case is a respected doctor
with very high references
and you know he would not
cause trouble in the
neighborhood. Would you
sell to him in that case
if you had a choice?

1. Yes
5. No

*Ask everyone*

F. Now reverse the situation. Suppose a close neighbor was selling his house
and he had a black customer for it. What would you want him to do: sell
to the customer or not sell?

1. Sell
2. Not sell
3. Wouldn't care, up to him
   (*volunteered*)

G.  Suppose a white home owner would be willing to sell his home to a black but feels he cannot because his neighbors would object. He explains the situation in a frank and friendly way to the black, saying that he himself would be willing to sell, but he doesn't want to cause his neighbors so much worry. If you heard about this, would you feel anything particular toward the home owner or the black?

H.  If answer to G was "none", ask: Would you have any feelings at all about the situation?
   If answer to G was unclear, ask: Would you have any other feelings?

**47.  Suppose you heard the house next door was being sold to a black family. Which *one* of the following characteristics would you most hope the black family moving in would have? [show card, read alternatives, and check 1st choice].

A.  Which characteristic would you *next* prefer in a black family moving next door? (check second choice)

                              47. First Choice     A. Second Choice

1. College graduate
2. Quiet and agreeable
3. Is a leader in solving
   neighborhood problems
4. Has well-behaved
   children
5. Friendly and outgoing
6. Keep up their house
   and yard

48.  Suppose there is a community-wide vote on the general housing issue. There are two possible laws to vote on:

1. *One law* says that a homeowner can decide for himself who to sell his house to, even if he prefers not to sell to blacks.
2. The *second law* says that a homeowner can*not* refuse to sell to someone because of their race or color.

Which law would you vote for?

| 1. First Law | 2. Second Law | 3. Neither |
|---|---|---|
| (*ask A*) | (*ask A*) | (*volunteered*) |
| | | (*skip to B*) |

A. If someone asked you to sign a petition that would be made public supporting the law you favor, would you be willing to sign it?

        1. Yes

        5. No

*Ask everyone*

B. Which law do you think your neighbors right around here would want you to vote for? (repeat laws if needed)

| 1. First Law | 2. Second Law | 3. Neighbors disagree among selves (*volunteered*) (*specify*) |
|---|---|---|
| 4. Neither (*volunteered*) (*ask C*) | 5. They wouldn't care (*volunteered*) (*ask C*) | |

C. Which law do you think most of the neighbors would vote for themselves?

        1. First Law

        2. Second Law

*Ask everyone*

D. Now reverse the situation. Which law would *you* want your neighbors right around here to vote for? (repeat laws if needed)

        1. First Law

        2. Second Law

        3. Neither (*volunteered*)

        4. Wouldn't care (*volunteered*)

49. Suppose there was a proposal at your children's school to give black parents an opportunity to transfer in about 25 black children from a very overcrowded school. The principal of your school calls a meeting of all parents to decide on the proposal and you go to the meeting. [if R says he doesn't have children, ask him to imagine he did] Would you support or oppose the proposal at the meeting?

| 1. Support (*ask A*) | 2. Oppose | 3. Not Vote |
|---|---|---|
| | | (*volunteered*) |

A. Suppose several very worried friends come to you before the meeting and urge you *not* to support the transfer because they are concerned about what it may do to the school and to the education of their children. Would you be willing to change your vote to avoid causing them worry, or at least not to vote at all?

          1. Yes, would change or not vote

          5. No, would not change

50. One day a six-year-old asks her mother if she can bring another girl home to play. The mother knows that the other girl is a black, and that her own daughter has only played with white children before. What should the mother do? Here are three possible responses. [read each and circle R's choice]

1. She should tell her daughter that she must never play with blacks
2. The daughter should be told that she may play with black children in school, but not at home
3. The black child should be permitted to come to the home

A. Do you think that most people *in the Detroit Area* would agree with you on what should be done about this?

  1. Yes             5. No (*ask B*)

          B. What would they choose? (reread three alternatives if needed)
            1. Never play
            2. Play at school only
            3. Play at home

C. How about most people *in this* neighborhood: Do you think they would agree with you on what should be done about this?

1. Yes   3. Neighbors would disagree among themselves (*volunteered*) (*specify*)   5. No (*ask D*)

D. What would they choose? (Reread alternatives if necessary)
1. Never play
2. Play at school only
3. Play at home

E. Suppose the white mother told her daughter that blacks were all right, but that it was better not to invite the girl home because it might lead to problems with white friends. Do you think the average black mother, if she learned of this, would be upset, *or* do you think she would understand the problems involved?

    1. Upset

    2. Understand

51. Suppose a good black engineer applied for a job as an engineering executive. The Personnel Director explained to him: "Personally I'd never give your race a thought, but the two men you would have to work with most closely—the plant manager and the chief engineer—both have strong feelings about blacks. I *can* offer you a job as a regular engineer, but *not* at the executive level, because any serious friction at the top could ruin the organization.

    A. Was it all right for the personnel director in this case to refuse to hire the black engineer as an executive in order to avoid friction with the other employees?

        1. Yes

        5. No

    B. Should the personnel manager have asked the other men how they would feel about working with a black engineer and then made his decision on the basis of their wishes?

        1. Yes

        5. No

    C. In general, do you think employers should hire men for top management without paying any attention to whether they are white or black?

        1. Yes

        5. No

52. Now I'd like you to imagine the following things happening. Please tell me how *you* would feel personally, even though you might not object openly. [if R replies in terms of what he would do or not do, repeat phrase about *"feel personally . . ."*]

    A. If you went to a house party and discovered that several black couples were there, would you personally mind a lot, a little, or not at all?

        1. Lot

        2. Little

        3. Not at all

        4. Would like it

          (*volunteered*)

B. If a very close relative went on a date with a black, would you mind a lot, a little, or not at all?

1. Lot
2. Little
3. Not at all
4. Would like it
   (*volunteered*)

C. If a very close relative married a black, would you mind a lot, a little, or not at all?

1. Lot
2. Little
3. Not at all
4. Would like it
   (*volunteered*)

53. On *all* the racial issues we've been discussing, do people who are close to you usually agree with your general views, or do they disagree—for example:

[*if married*]
A. How about your (husband's/wife's) views: would you say they are more favorable toward blacks than yours, the same as yours, or less favorable?

1. More favorable
2. Same
3. Less favorable

[*ask everyone*]
B. Do you think your closest friends' views are more favorable toward blacks than yours, about the same as yours, or less favorable than yours?

1. More favorable
2. Same
3. Less favorable

[*ask everyone*]
C. Do you think the views of your parents would be more favorable toward blacks than yours, about the same as yours, or less favorable? [if parents deceased, ask what theirs would be if alive today]

1. More favorable
2. Same
3. Less favorable

D. If R has any children age 14 and over [inquire, if necesssary]
How about your children's views: are they more favorable than yours, the same as yours, or less favorable?

1. More favorable
2. Same
3. Less favorable

E. [Fill in blanks from Q. 3 on p. 1]
You mentioned earlier that the national leaders you admire most
are _____ and _____. Would you say their views toward
blacks are more favorable than yours, about the same as yours, or less
favorable than yours?

    1. More favorable    2. Same    3. Less favorable
                        8. Don't know (*ask A*)
                        A. What would be your best
                            guess on that?
                            1. More favorable
                            2. Same
                            3. Less favorable
                            8. Don't know
                              (accept if volunteered)

F. If *nobody* in A, B, C, or D is mentioned as more favorable than R, ask:
Do you know anyone personally whose views toward blacks are more
favorable than yours?

                1. Yes
                5. No

One final set of questions on race has to do with any actual contacts you may
have had with blacks.

54. In the two or three blocks right around her, how many of the families, if
any, are black: none, only a few, many but less than half, or more than half?

    1. None    2. Only a few    3. Many but less    4. More than half
                (*ask A & B*)       than half       half (*ask A & B*)
                                (*ask A & B*)

*If any blacks*
A. Do you and the black families that live around here visit in each other's
homes, *or* do you only see and talk to each other on the street, *or* do
you hardly know each other?

    1. Visit in each    2. See and talk    3. Hardly know
        other's home        on the street        them

B. Do any of these black families live within five or six houses of yours?

                1. Yes
                5. No

55. Apart from neighbors, are there (other) blacks, including people from work, that you get together with socially or in recreational activities?
    1. Yes (*ask A*)         5. No

    A. Could you give a recent example
       of the kind of activity you mean?

56. When you were growing up, were there any black families living in or near your neighborhood?
           1. Yes
           5. No

57. In all the years you went to school, did you ever go to a school where there were black students too?
    1. Yes (*ask A*)         5. No

    A. How many black students were there (in the school that had most); few, less than half, half, or more than half?
           1. Few blacks
           2. Less than half
           3. About half
           4. More than half

**58. At the present some black neighborhoods have schools with rundown buildings and less trained teachers than schools in mainly white neighborhoods. Do you think the federal government should provide more money to bring these black schools up to the standard of the white schools, or that the government shouldn't do this?
           1. Should
           2. Should not

Now I'd like to turn to questions on other subjects.
59. When you were growing up, would you say your family was fairly well-off financially, about average, or did they have to struggle pretty hard to make ends meet?
           1. Fairly well-off
           2. Average
           3. Had to struggle hard

60. How about yourself today: would you say you are fairly well-off financially, average, or do you sometimes have trouble making ends meet?
           1. Well-off
           2. Average
           3. Trouble making ends meet

61. Do you and your family own this (home/apartment), rent it, or what?
    1. Own or buying
    2. Rent
    3. Other (*specify*)

62. Interviewer note: (*circle appropriate category*)
    1. R is head of household and male
    2. R is head of household and female
    3. R is wife of head

    *N.B.* : Ask 62 A-G about *Head's* job.

A. (One of the things we are interested in is the kind of work people in Detroit do.) What is your (your husband's) main job at the present time? Probe carefully for specific job: obtain formal job title where possible. If *retired* or *unemployed*, indicate clearly, then ask about "last main job."

B. What kind of business is (was) that in? (*e.g., steelmill, bank, etc.*)

C. Do you (does he) work for yourself (himself) or for someone else?
    1. Self
    2. Someone else

D. Do you (does your husband) belong to a Union?
    1. Yes        5. No

E. What Union is that?

F. (Do you/does your husband) work at a second job ten hours a week or more?
    1. Yes
    5. No

G. (Have you/has your husband) been unemployed at anytime in the past five years when (you/he) didn't want to be? [don't count illness or strikes]
    1. Yes
    5. No

*Ask wives only*
63. Do you yourself work at a job 10 hours or more a week?
    1. Yes
    5. No
    0. INAP: R is not a wife

*Ask working heads and working wives*
64. Of the 10 or 12 people you work most closely with on your job, are there any blacks?
    1. Yes (*ask A, B, & C.*)    5. No

    A. How many are blacks?


    B. Are there any differences in the way blacks and whites at the same level job do their work?
       1. Yes (*ask C*)    5. No

    C. What sort of differences?




[*Ask everyone*]
65. What (is/was) your father's main job or occupation?


    A. What kind of business (industry, organization) (is/was) that in?

    B. (Does/Did) he work for himself or for someone else?
               1. Self
               2. Someone else

66. How many years of school did your father *complete*? (*check below*)

67. How many years of school did *you yourself complete*? (*check below*)

[*If married*]
68. How many years of school did your (husband/wife) *complete*? (*check below*)

|  | 66. Father | 67. Self | 68. Spouse |
|---|---|---|---|
| 1. Less than 8th grade |  |  |  |
| 2. 8th grade |  |  |  |
| 3. Some high school (9-11 grades) |  |  |  |
| 4. Finished high school (12th grade) |  |  |  |
| 5. Some college |  |  |  |
| 6. College graduate or more |  |  |  |

69. What country did most of your ancestors come from? (if R says "America," say: What country did they come from before coming to America?)

70. How many children do you have, whether living here or elsewhere? Include all children, whether living at home or not, whether own, adopted, etc. Do *not* include deceased.

No. of Children (*if any, ask A & B*)

A. [If any children] Could you please tell me their ages from the youngest to the oldest?

Ages from Oldest to Youngest

[If any children]
B. How many are living here?
children living at home

71. What is your own age, please?

72. Does anyone else live here at present?
1. Yes (*ask A*)                    5. No

A. Obtain relation of each to head, and sex of each
Relation to Head                Sex

73. Do you have a religious preference; that is, are you Protestant, Catholic, Jewish, or something else.

1. Protestant (and what denomination is that)?
2. Catholic
3. Jewish
4. None
7. Other (specify)

74. About how often did you attend religious services during the last year? (show card and read choices)
1. Never
2. Once or twice a year
3. Several times a year

4. At least once a month
5. 2 or 3 times a month
6. Once a week
7. Twice a week
8. More than twice a week

75. *If ever attends church*

Does your minister devote sermons and other time to preaching on social problems such as race relations, or does he concentrate almost entirely on spiritual and moral concerns?

1. Social problems
2. Spiritual and moral

76. *If R has any religion*

Here are several statements that some people have made about their feelings toward religion. For each one, would you tell me whether you agree or disagree—that is, whether or not the statement is true for you also.

|  | Agree | Disagree |
|---|---|---|
| A. The most important thing that religion offers me is comfort when sorrow and misfortune strike. | | |
| B. The purpose of prayer is to secure a happy and peaceful life. | | |
| C. It is important to me to spend periods of time in private religious thought and prayer. | | |
| D. My religious beliefs are what really lie behind my whole approach to life. | | |

77. About what was your *total family income* last year [1968] before taxes, for you and your family, including *all* sources such as wages, profits, interest, and so on. [hand card] Just give me the letter on the card that fits.

(A)  01. Under $4,000
(B)  02. $4,000 to 5,999
(C)  03. $6,000 to 7,999
(D)  04. $8,000 to 9,999
(E)  05. $10,000 to 11,999
(F)  06. $12,000 to 13,999
(G)  07. $14,000 to 16,999
(H)  08. $17,000 to 19,999
(I)  09. Over $20,000

78. Thinking about your total family income would you say you are very satisfied, fairly satisfied, somewhat dissatisfied, or very dissatisfied?
    1. Very satisfied
    2. Fairly satisfied
    3. Somewhat dissatisfied
    4. Very dissatisfied

79. Generally speaking, do you usually think of yourself as a Republican, a Democrat, or what?
    1. Republican (*ask A*)  2. Democrat (*ask A*)   3. Independent (*ask B*)

A. Do you consider yourself a strong (Democrat/Republican) or not a very strong (Democrat/Republican)?

    1. Strong    2. Not Strong

B. Do you generally lean more toward the Republican or Democratic party?

    1. Lean Republican
    2. Lean Democrat
    3. Neither (*volunteered*)
       [R is not closer to one party or the other]

80. Do you think your own views are more *liberal* or more conservative than those of the Democratic party generally, or would you say that you're *not sure*?
    1. More liberal
    2. Same as party (*volunteered*)
    3. More conservative
    8. Not sure or don't know

81. How about the Republicans? Do you think your own views are generally more *liberal* or more *conservative* than those of the Republican party, or would you say you're *not sure*?
    1. More liberal
    2. Same as party (*volunteered*)
    3. More conservative
    8. Not sure or don't know

X. That finishes the interview. Is there anything you would like to add to any of the subjects we've discussed?

Y. May I have your phone number in case my office wants to verify this interview?

Phone No.

*Time ended:

Z. *Hand post-interview questionnaire.* This sheet asks you to indicate what you thought of the interview. Would you please fill it out after I'm gone and mail it to the University in this stamped envelope.

122

Interviewer: Fill this out immediately *before* leaving neighborhood. *Essential*

200. Total interview time in minutes: (do not include time spent talking with R after interview is officially over.)     minutes

201. Respondent's understanding of questions:
    1. Excellent understanding     2. Good     3. Fair     4. Poor

202. Did the respondent ever suggest that (her/his) views on racial issues differ from yours?
    1. Yes (Code A & B)               5. No

    A. On what questions did this occur?



    B. Did the respondent suggest he saw himself as being more liberal or more conservative on race than you?
    1. More liberal on race
    2. More conservative on race
    7. Other (Specify)

203. Was the respondent defensive about any of (his/her) racial answers?
    1. Yes                           5. No

204. How often on the racial questions did R reject the question as worded and attempt to make distinctions (between middle class and working class black or white, between young and old, etc.)?
    1. Often        2. Occasionally        3. Rarely        4. Never

205. After the first few questions on race were you able to predict all, almost all, most, or very few of the rest of the respondent's answers to racial questions?
    1. All          2. Almost all          3. Most          4. Very few

206. How much did you personally like the interview?
    1. A great deal    2. Somewhat        3. It was all right but
                                             I did not especially enjoy it
                       4. Disliked the interview

207. Did R ever show evidence of emotional hositility toward blacks? How?

208. Did R ever use any racial terms other than white and black? What terms did he use?

209. What persons over 10 years of age were present during the interview? (check all present)
    1. None        2. Spouse of R        3. Child over 10
                7. Other (*specify*)
  A. [*If anyone else present*]
    Did this affect the interview in any important way? How?

210. Please give here a brief description of the respondent, and of any special conditions that affected the interview.

[Space for Continuations: Be sure to give Q. No.]

# Appendix B:
# The Measurement of the
# Liberalism-Conservatism
# Dimension

In regard to the validity of our measure of ideology, it is often the case that questions with a very high "don't know" rate are deleted. A high "don't know" rate does raise doubts about the meaningfulness of the question. A related problem is that a large percentage of those who answer the question may do so in order to give a desirable response. What do individual respondents mean when they do use the terms liberal or conservative? Respondents might be relating to only a single aspect or issue of the liberalism-conservatism polarity. The parties themselves are inconsistent, combining liberal views in some areas with conservative policies in other areas. It may be argued that we are projecting various arenas of meaning on a measure of the overall understanding of liberalism-conservatism which may or may not be valid for the respondents.

In answer to these criticisms we feel, in the first place, that based upon what we already know, one would expect to find only a minority of the sample able to relate consistently to liberal-conservative distinctions. That approximately 60 percent of respondents are unable to say whether their own position is more or less conservative than the major parties confirms the meaninglessness—the lack of clarity—of the conventional dimension for the electorate. The inability to relate to either party, then (expressed through the "don't know" response rate) is a substantive response that is relevant to our investigation. Of course it may be suggested that we are not accurately capturing that small percentage of the population who are ideologues. That we are at the very least measuring those respondents who are more aware is substantiated by selected social background factors.

Another question is raised after examination of the distribution of respondents on the liberalism-conservatism dimension relative to the Republican and Democratic parties. Why are so many respondents found to be more liberal or more conservative than both parties, while so few occupy the same position as the major parties? First, "about the same" was not an alternative phrased in the question. In pretests a "same" category seemed to be used by respondents as a middle or neutral category. Therefore, this alternative was deleted from the schedule so as to leave this as a voluntary response.

The noticeable decline in the proportion of ideologues from the pretests to the final survey could reasonably be attributed in part to this deletion. Therefore, the present "same" category is quite a conservative estimate of those respondents belonging here. We found the "same" respondents to be a homogeneous social grouping, readily differentiated from the other subgroups on a wide variety of SES and attitude items. In sum, we did not want to encourage nonideologues to use ideological labels that were meaningless to them.

A further rationale for the conservative use of the "same" category was to maximize the number of respondents in extreme positions. Although some respondents may have been accurately placed in the liberal and conservative groups, we feared that there might be too few extremists to justify analysis. More than five years ago in fact, Segal (1968b), in a proposal to the Detroit Area Study Executive Committee, suggested that the sample be stratified so as to "overrepresent the economically and socially 'marginal' middle class, viz., small businessmen and college professors. . . ." Certainly, a particular coding scheme cannot overcome sampling difficulties. However, we are prepared at this point in the development of these instruments to risk maximizing the extreme subgroups on the basis of the optimistic expectation that the central tendencies of the subgroups are sufficiently different to enable us to meaningfully contrast them. On the basis of the results, our expectation of such differentiation is tentatively confirmed.

The fact that we did find respondents who fall to the left or right of both major parties surely detracted from the size of the "same" positions. On the other hand, this approach may reflect reality and so explain why so many voters are commonly, yet mistakenly, thought to occupy the same position as the parties. The very nature of ideology seems to imply that those in party positions are not likely to be ideologues (except for party officials). To be an ideologue is to have more than the usual level of political sophistication. In a system where the ideological appeals of the party appear to be quite limited, ideologues are not likely to be those who strongly identify with the major parties, but those who perhaps through higher education have become more sensitized to the liberalism-conservatism dimension.

**Notes**

# Notes

## Notes to Chapter 1

1. The book by Campbell et al. (1960), is undoubtedly a major contribution to our understanding of the American electorate. Converse's article (1964) has similarly influenced all research done in the area of political belief systems.

2. Our operationalization of ideology is based on the respondent's use of liberal-conservative labels.

3. Much of the relevant literature in social psychology is largely unintegrated into the study of political sociology. Since there is no complete model for analysis of belief systems available, we must attempt to go beyond present limitations.

4. *Sampling Memorandum for DAS 981*, November 1969, Detroit Area Study (mimeo).

5. As a Survey Research Center *Technical Report* appearing in 1969 documents, "In general, refusals have doubled from 5 to 6 percent of the sample to 10 or 11 percent ... the increase in refusals has been larger both in absolute and relative terms for larger cities."

6. The Survey Research Center interviewers achieved a considerably higher response rate than did the student interviewers.

7. See Appendix B for a discussion of measurement difficulties.

8. This suggests within certain confidence limits the meaninglessness of liberalism-conservatism for the vast majority of those responding. Some of the confusion created by not allowing for a same category in the wording of the question might partially account for 9 percent of the ideologues being inconsistent.

## Notes to Chapter 2

1. Table 1-3 (Chapter 1) outlines those positions which are logically possible.

2. The term "beyond the poles" will be used to refer to those ideologues who are more extreme than the major parties. That there are segments of the electorate beyond the polar positions for whom it may be just as easy to move toward the support of one extremist candidate as to support a presidential candidate representing the opposite extreme is substantiated by findings from the 1968 election. Wolfe (1969) found that among Democratic identifiers who voted for Wallace, nearly one-quarter preferred McCarthy and another one-quarter preferred Kennedy. Although they may not have *voted* for McCarthy or Kennedy, this result "at least raises the possibility of some interesting alterna-

tives in candidate preference which certainly do not fit on a traditional left-right ideological dimension" (Wolfe, 1969:7).

These Democratic identifiers might lead one to suggest that positions beyond the strong partisan locations may perhaps represent a "threshold," such that some of those beyond the poles are less constrained by the logic of the left-right dimension. Those beyond the poles may, under certain conditions, it seems, support a candidate of either extreme or a moderate. Some groups that are left of left could vote for Democratic candidates such as McGovern or Robert F. Kennedy, or perhaps Republican candidates such as Rockefeller or Lindsay. However, more extreme groups such as the S.D.S. are not likely to be pulled into the Democratic fold at all.

3. This measures 22 percent of the sample. Converse (1964:222) finds 17 percent of the electorate to relate to a broad philosophy as indicated by the "best answers" to the liberalism-conservatism distinction. These percentages are close if one considers the different measurement techniques and sampling differences.

**Notes to Chapter 3**

1. The finding that Republicans are overrepresented among the ideologue group is compatible with the fact that ideologues tend to be of higher socioeconomic status than nonideologues.

2. As a measure of statistical significance, the conventional .05 level for $Chi^2$ will be used unless otherwise stated.

3. This question was presented later in the interview referring specifically to poorer *black* schools. Different parts of the sample were asked these alternative questions. This more general question was asked of only 137 respondents, the remaining 503 respondents being asked their opinion on federal support of poorer black schools.

4. This Detroit Area Study Index is constructed from the following three items:

How about crimes such as robbery and assault in the Detroit area—would you say almost all such crimes are committed by blacks, about half, or less than half?

| Category | New Value |
|---|---|
| Almost all by blacks | 3 |
| More than half | 2 |
| About half, less than half | 1 |

Do you think the victims of black crimes are mostly black or mostly white?

| Category | New Value |
|---|:---:|
| Mostly black | 1 |
| Mostly white | 3 |
| Half and half | 2 |

How much danger, if any, do you think there is of groups of blacks from the inner city going out to white areas and suburbs to commit violence on whites?

A minimum-maximum score of (3-9)–2 yields a range of 1-7. No missing data are allowed. The correlations between the three items are significant at the .01 level. In this and other indices only items correlated with a probability $< .01$ were included.

5. Ambiguous or vague responses, such as "all we can do is pray," we treated as missing data. The answers stressing a positive response range from efforts to "give Negroes self-respect," to eliminating discrimination in education, employment, and housing. The repressive answers mention police power and range from "separatism" to "harsher treatment for rioters."

6. The index of social distance was created with the following codes.

| | | | |
|---|---|:---:|:---:|
| Black at party: | Mind a lot | = | 3 |
| Relative date black: | Mind a little | = | 2 |
| Relative marry black: | Not at all | = | 1 |
| Play with black child: | Never | = | 3 |
| | School | = | 2 |
| | Home | = | 1 |

The resulting scale ranged from 1-9 [(4 12)=3 = 1-9].

A score of 1 indicates that the respondent did not object at all to interracial contact, and a score of 9 implies high social distance on all four questions.

7. That some social psychologists have also adopted the left-right cleavage is exemplified in the work of Adorno et al. Throughout the investigation, a liberal-conservative scale of attitudes is implicit.

8. These various aspects of the externalization syndrome like the liberalism-conservatism dimension may be seen as constraints on political consciousness.

9. All indices are constructed by summing responses. Where items are not worded so that agreement carries the same meaning, the response on the item is reversed and then responses are summed. Again, no missing data are allowed.

## Notes to Chapter 5

1. James admits that there may be "some miniscule minority of true independents who fit the popular stereotype ... but they are not numerous

enough to seriously modify the weak qualification of Independents as voters" (James, 1969:87). James also reasons that since "V.O. Key stressed the rationality of voters who switched from one party's candidate to the other in successive elections. . . . Independents are not the same as 'switchers.' "

2. The traditional cross-pressure argument adds to the explanation of political identification. The argument that voters withdraw from party affiliation due to cross-pressures supports the conception of Independents as middle-of-the-roaders. "Persons in group cross-pressure are less likely to participate than those not cross-pressured" (Milbrath, 1965:132). The debate on whether those persons who are cross-pressured withdraw to a central position, or even whether they are in fact less likely to participate needs further investigation.

3. Implicit in the predominant literature, we feel, is the notion that the role of the Independent (as a middle-of-the-roader) is a functional one. However, if one simply observes the political activities on any large university campus, much of the political meaning of Independence shifts to "beyond the poles." Many educated youths may identify themselves as Independents out of a desire to register their protests against the system. Under certain conditions, the Independent vote could become dysfunctional for the system. For example, status inconsistents, with a high ascribed status but a low achieved status, might be attracted to parties of the right such as the A.I.P., or to candidates backed by the John Birch Society.

4. Often we find extremism and independence defined as mutually exclusive categories, or we hear the statement that a political actor is either an extremist *or* an Independent—implying that the political spectrum is like this:

Extremist — Democrat — Independent — Republican — Extremist

However, as our data indicate, there are *extremist Independents.*

5. Stokes (1966) has suggested that most spatial interpretations of party competition have a "very poor fit with the evidence about how large-scale electorates and political leaders actually respond to politics." In particular he questions four assumptions: (1) the unidimensionality of the left-right space, (2) the stability of the structure in which parties compete, (3) the existence of an ordered issue dimension, and (4) the common frame of reference of parties and electorate.

6. Campbell et al. (1960:135), speak of the "enduring role of partisan commitment in shaping attitudes toward political objects."

7. There is most definitely covariance among age, marital status, and home ownership.

8. A 1968 Gallup survey of college students found 43 percent describing themselves as Independents. The 1969 survey found 44 percent of college students to be Independents (Gallup Opinion Index, 1968, 1969).

9. As Ladd (1970:310) indicates, "In the late 1960s the percentage calling themselves Independents among twenty-one- and twenty-nine-year-olds in-

creased sharply, and all major surveys for the first time reported Independents outnumbering both Democrats and Republicans."

## Notes to Chapter 6

1. The specific program used was G-L SSAI, now Minissa I.

2. The coefficient of alienation may be seen as equivalent to a measure of the unexplained variance, $\sqrt{1-r^2}$. Therefore, the correspondence between the data and its graphic representation must be very high ($r = .99$) to achieve such a fit.

3. The question with the lowest number of cases ($N = 460$) asks respondents about their opinion on federal support of poorer black schools. This question was selected over the more general question regarding federal support of poor schools due to the larger N.

4. Since the coefficient of alienation can be represented by $\sqrt{1-r^2}$ to achieve coefficients of .20 and .18, r must equal .980 and .984 respectively.

## Notes to Chapter 7

1. We are assuming that all voters who feel that they occupy the same ideological position as their party will be equally likely to vote for the party regardless of the strength of their partisan affect, i.e., regardless of whether they are strong partisans, weak partisans, Independents leaning toward the party, or Independents of no leaning. Also, for purposes of estimating maximum change in the electoral market through ideological change on the part of the parties, we assume that there is only one liberal position to the left of both parties, one conservative position to the right of them, and one middle-of-the-road position between them. This being the case, we would, for example, expect that if the Democratic party moved to the liberal position, all liberal groups would be aggregated to form a new Democratic organizational bloc ($< 6\%$ strong Democrats $+ < 6\%$ weak Democrats $+ 3\%$ Independents of Democratic leaning $+ 7\%$ Independents of no leaning $= 21\%$).

2. As Katz (1960) submits, one of the functions of attitudes is that of value expression; the other functions being knowledge, ego defensive and adjustive functions. We believe there is reason to see this value-expressive function of attitudes as the dominant function. If this is the case, then the examination of values is of considerable significance. Rokeach (1969b:132) provides the basis for this approach in his suggestion that "the knowledge, ego-defensive, and adjustive functions all involve central values." Value expression as the most general function of attitudes can be seen as mediating between the more specific ego-defense mechanisms, etc., and central values. More accurately, we might

conceive of the knowledge, ego-defensive, and adjustive processes as three more or less distinct clusters of values.

3. The same values which produce systemic strains are also those which underlie the stability of the American political system. The pervasiveness of the value of freedom which has meant incredible economic progress has also led to racial conflicts which can be seen as largely attempts to bypass obstacles placed in the path of blacks in their pursuit of a freer life.

4. The paucity of ideology which has been recently made so much of in the "end of ideology" debate, can be explained by this agreement on basic social values. One might well argue that the end of ideology question is misdirected, since Americans were never prone to articulateness in political theorizing. Speaking of the Civil War, Boorstin (1953:131) comments, "This, the bloodiest single civil war of the nineteenth century, was also perhaps the least theoretical." Similarly, for Hartz, even the protests of labor in the 1930s, and the New Deal itself, were not oriented towards achievement of collectivist goals, but were motivated by a concern for increasing participation within the system as constituted. The same is largely true of the civil rights movement.

5. Rokeach (1969a, 1969b, 1971, 1973) and his associates have found in their research that primary differences in values for various political orientations are very few.

6. Values form a hierarchy. They may conflict and the centrality of one value over another determines which value will win out (Rokeach, 1969a). In the case of freedom and equality, the distance between freedom and equality is what matters—for if the distance is great, freedom is less tempered with a concern for equality.

7. The Democratic party, for example, could move a larger number of Southern blacks into their fold. Related to and underlying the reluctance of party leaders regarding ideological appeals is the fact that American parties are not mass membership organizations. Major parties don't utilize formal procedures to attract a mass membership. As Campbell et al. put it, "Generally this tie is a psychological identification, which can (and most often does) persist without legal recognition or evidence of formal membership and even without a consistent record of party support" (1960:121).

8. The success of the two-party system in spite of the muted ideological appeals can be understood to rest on the very consensus regarding social values. Since there is a "universal consciousness" about central values, party leaders can supply voters with only the vaguest clues about policy questions. Rokeach suggests a technique for evaluating the probability of a person voting for a particular candidate based on the individual's perception of the centrality of equality for the candidate. "It is reasonable to assume that political candidates running for public office have differing value systems and that their appeal to the voter will depend on the degree of congruence between candidate and voter value systems" (Rokeach, 1969a:558).

# Bibliography

# Bibliography

Adorno, T.W., Else Frenkel-Brunswik, Daniel J. Levinson, and R.N. Sanford. *The Authoritarian Personality*. New York: Harper, 1950.

Alford, Robert R. *Party and Society*. Chicago: Rand McNally, 1963.

Alford, Robert R., and Harry M. Scoble. "Sources of Local Political Involvement." *American Political Science Review* 62 (December): 1192-1206, 1968.

Almond, Gabriel A., and Sidney Verba. *The Civic Culture*. Princeton: Princeton University Press, 1963.

Allport, Gordon. "The Composition of Political Attitudes." *American Journal of Sociology* 35:220-238, 1929.

_____. *The Nature of Prejudice*. Cambridge, Mass.: Addison-Wesley, 1954.

Asch, Solomon E. *Social Psychology*. Englewood Cliffs, N.J.: Prentice-Hall, 1952.

Axelrod, Robert. "The Structure of Public Opinion on Policy Issues." *Public Opinion Quarterly* 31 (Spring): 51-60, 1967.

Bell, Daniel. *The End of Ideology*. New York: Free Press, 1965.

Berelson, Bernard R., Paul F. Lazarsfeld, and William N. McPhee. *Voting*. Chicago: University of Chicago Press, 1954.

Bobrow, Davis B. "Organization of American National Security Opinion." *Public Opinion Quarterly* 33 (Summer): 223-239, 1969.

Boorstin, Daniel J. *The Genius of American Politics*. Chicago: University of Chicago Press, 1953.

Bowles, Roy T., and James T. Richardson. "Sources of Consistency of Political Opinion." *American Journal of Sociology* 74 (May): 676-684, 1969.

Brown, Steven K. "Consistency and the Persistence of Ideology: Some Experimental Results." *Public Opinion Quarterly* (Spring): 60-68, 1970.

Buchanan, James M. and Gordon Tullock. *The Calculus of Consent*. Ann Arbor. University of Michigan Press, 1965.

Campbell, Angus. "The Passive Citizen." *Acta Sociologica* 6: 9-21, 1962.

Campbell, Angus, Philip E. Converse, Warren E. Miller, and Donald E. Stokes. *The American Voter*. New York: John Wiley & Sons, Inc., 1960.

Campbell, Angus, Gerald Gurin, and Warren E. Miller. *The Voter Decides*. Evanston, Ill.: Row, Peterson, 1954.

Campbell, Angus, and Henry Valen. "Party Identification in Norway and the United States" (pp. 245-268). In Angus Campbell, Philip E. Converse, Warren E. Miller and Donald E. Stokes (Eds.) *Elections and the Political Order*. New York: John Wiley & Sons, Inc., 1964.

Converse, Philip E. "Information Flow and the Stability of Partisan Attitudes." *Public Opinion Quarterly* 26 (Winter): 578-599, 1962.

_____. "The Nature of Belief Systems in Mass Publics." In David E. Apter (Ed.) *Ideology and Discontent*. © 1964 Free Press of Glencoe, Collier-Macmillan Limited.

Converse, Philip E. "The Problem of Party Distances in Models of Voting Change" (pp. 175-207). In M. Kent Jennings and L. Harmon Zeigler (Eds.) *The Electoral Process*. Englewood Cliffs, N.J.: Prentice-Hall, 1966.

_____. "Of Time and Partisan Stability." *Comparative Political Studies* (July): 139-171, 1969.

Converse, Philip E., and George Dupeux. "Politicization of the Electorate in France and the United States." *Public Opinion Quarterly* 26 (Spring): 1-24, 1962.

Converse, Philip E., Warren E. Miller, Jerold G. Rusk, and A.C. Wolfe. "Continuity and Change in American Politics: Parties and Issues in the 1968 Election." *American Political Science Review* 63 (December): 1083-1105, 1969.

Conway, M. Margaret, and Frank B. Feigert. "Motivation, Incentive Systems, and the Political Party Organization." *American Political Science Review* 62 (December): 1159-1173, 1968.

Cox, Kevin R. "The Spatial Structuring of Information Flow and Partisan Attitudes." In Mattei Dogan and Stein Rokkan (Eds.) *Quantitative Ecological Analysis in the Social Sciences*. Cambridge, Mass.: M.I.T. Press, 1969.

Cutright, P. and Peter H. Rossi. "Grass Roots Politicians and the Vote." *American Sociological Review* 23: 171-179, 1958.

Davis, Otto A., Melvin J. Hinich, and Peter C. Ordeshook. "An Expository Development of a Mathematical Model of the Electoral Process." *American Political Science Review* 64 (June): 426-448, 1970.

Davis, Otto A., and Melvin J. Hinich. "On the Power and Importance of the Mean Preference in a Mathematical Model of Democratic Choice," *Graduate School of Industrial Administration*, Reprint # 399, Carnegie-Mellon University, Pa., 1968.

Downs, Anthony. *An Economic Theory of Democracy*. New York: Harper and Row, 1957.

Duncan, Otis Dudley. "The Trend of Occupational Mobility in the United States." *American Sociological Review* 30 (August): 491-498, 1965.

Duverger, Maurice. *Political Parties*. New York: John Wiley, 1963.

Easton, David, and J. Dennis. "The Child's Acquisition of Regime Norms: Political Efficacy." *American Political Science Review* 61 (March): 25-38, 1967.

Eldersveld, Samuel J. *Political Parties: A Behavioral Analysis*. Chicago: Rand McNally, 1964.

Elizur, Dov. *Adapting to Innovation: A Facet Analysis of the Case of the Computer*. Jerusalem: Jerusalem Academic Press, 1969.

Eysenck, Hans J. *The Psychology of Politics*. London: Routledge and Kegan Paul, 1954.

Ferguson, Leonard W. "Primary Social Attitudes." *Journal of Psychology* 8: 217-223, 1939.

Ferguson, Leonard W. "The Measurement of Primary Social Attitudes." *Journal of Psychology* 10: 199-205, 1940.

_____. "A Revision of the Primary Social Attitude Scales." *Journal of Psychology* 17: 229-241, 1944.

Fishel, Jeff. "Party, Ideology, and the Congressional Challenger." *American Political Science Review* 63 (December): 1213-1232, 1969.

Flanigan, William H. *Partisanship and Campaign Participation*. Unpublished Doctoral Dissertation: Yale University, 1961.

Gallup Opinion Index. 1968: 37, 1969: 38.

Garvey, Gerald. "The Theory of Party Equilibrium." *American Political Science Review* 60: 29-38, 1966.

Greenstein, Fred I. *Children and Politics*. New Haven: Yale University Press, 1966.

_____. *Personality and Politics*. Chicago: Markham, 1969.

Guttman, Louis. "A General Nonmetric Technique for Finding the Smallest Euclidean Space for a Configuration of Points." *Psychometrika* 33 (December): 469-509, 1968.

Guttman, Louis, and I.M. Schlesinger. "Smallest Space Analysis of Intelligence and Achievement Tests." *Psychological Bulletin* 71(2): 95-100, 1969.

Hartz, Louis. *The Liberal Tradition in America*. New York: Harcourt Brace Jovanovich, 1955.

Hennessy, Bernard. "A Headnote on the Existence and Study of Political Attitudes." *Social Science Quarterly* 51 (December): 463-476, 1970.

Hess, Robert D., and Judith V. Torney. *The Development of Political Attitudes in Children*. Garden City: Doubleday, 1968.

Hinich, Melvin J., and Peter C. Ordeshook. "Plurality Maximization vs. Vote Maximization: A Spatial Analysis with Variable Participation." *American Political Science Review* 64 (September): 772-91, 1970.

Hotelling, Harold. "Stability in Competition." *Economic Journal* 39: 41-57, 1929.

Hyman, Herbert H. *Political Socialization*. Glencoe, Ill.: Free Press, 1959.

Inglehart, Ronald, and Auram Hochstein. "Alignment and Dealignment of the Electorate in France and the United States." *Comparative Political Studies* 5 (October): 343-372, 1972.

Jahoda, Marie, and Neil Warren (Eds.) *Attitudes*. Middlesex, England: Penguin, 1966.

James, Judson L. *American Political Parties*, © 1969, by Western Publishing Company, Inc., reprinted by permission of The Bobbs-Merrill Company, Inc.

Jennings, M. Kent, and Harmon Zeigler. "The Salience of American State Politics." *American Political Science Review* 64 (June): 523-535, 1970.

Kariel, Henry S. "Creating Political Reality." *American Political Science Review* 64 (December): 1088-1098, 1970.

Katz, Daniel. "The Functional Approach to the Study of Attitudes." *Public Opinion Quarterly* 24: 163-204, 1960.

Katz, Daniel, and Samuel J. Eldersveld. "The Impact of Local Party Activity Upon the Electorate." *Public Opinion Quarterly* 25 (Spring): 1-24, 1961.

Katz, Daniel, and E. Stotland. "A Preliminary Statement to a Theory of Attitude Structure and Change" (pp. 423-475). In S. Koch (Ed.) *Psychology: A Study of a Science.* New York: McGraw-Hill, 1959.

Kerr, William A. "Correlates of Politico-Economic Liberalism-Conservatism." *Journal of Social Psychology* 20: 61-77, 1944.

_____. "Untangling the Liberalism-Conservatism Continuum." *Journal of Social Psychology* 35: 111-125, 1952.

Key, V.O., Jr. *Politics, Parties, and Pressure Groups.* New York: Crowell, 1958.

_____. *Public Opinion and American Democracy.* New York: Knopf, 1965.

_____. *The Responsible Electorate.* Cambridge, Mass.: Belknap Press, 1966.

_____. *Southern Politics.* New York: Knopf, 1969.

Ladd, Everett Carll. *Ideology in America.* Ithaca, N.Y.: Cornell University Press, 1969.

_____. *American Political Parties.* New York: W.W. Norton, 1970.

Lane, Robert E. *Political Life.* New York: Free Press, 1959.

_____. *Political Ideology: Why the Common Man Believes What He Does.* New York: Free Press, 1962.

_____. *Political Thinking and Consciousness: The Private Life of the Political Mind.* Chicago: Markham, 1969.

Langton, Kenneth P. *Political Socialization.* New York: Oxford University Press, 1969.

LaPonce, J.A. "Notes on the Use of the Left-Right Dimension." *Comparative Political Studies* 2 (January): 481-502, 1970.

Laumann, Edward O. *Prestige and Association in an Urban Community.* New York: Bobbs-Merrill, 1966.

_____. "The Social Structure of Ethnic Groups in a Metropolitan Community: A Smallest Space Analysis." *Working Paper #7: Detroit Area Study.* The University of Michigan, 1968.

Laumann, Edward O., and James S. House. "Living Room Styles and Social Attributes: The Patterning of Material Artifacts in a Modern Urban Community." *Sociology and Social Research* 54 (April): 321-342, 1970.

Laumann, Edward O., and David R. Segal. "Status Inconsistency and Ethno-religious Group Membership as Determinants of Social Participation and Political Attitudes." *American Journal of Sociology* 77 (July): 36-61, 1971.

Lazarsfeld, Paul, Bernard Berelson, and Hazel Gaudet. *The People's Choice.* New York: Columbia University Press, 1944.

Lenski, Gerhard E. *The Religious Factor.* Garden City, N.Y.: Doubleday, 1963.

Lentz, Theodore F. "The Attitudes of World Citizenship." *Journal of Social Psychology* 32: 207-214, 1950.

Levinson, D.J. "Conservatism and Radicalism." *International Encyclopedia of the Social Sciences.* New York: Macmillan, 1968.

Lewin, Kurt. *Field Theory in Social Science*. New York: Harper Torchbook, 1951.

Lingoes, James C. "A Multiple Scalogram Analysis of Selected Issues of the 83rd U.S. Senate." *American Psychologist* 17 (May): 327, 1962. Abstract of a paper read at the American Psychological Association August 1962.

_____. "The Multivariate Analysis of Qualitative Data." *Multivariate Behavioral Research* 3 (January): 61-94, 1968.

_____. "A General Survey of the Guttman-Lingoes Nonmetric Program Series." The University of Michigan, 1970a.

_____. "An I.B.M. 360/67 Program for Guttman-Lingoes Smallest Space Analysis." The University of Michigan, 1970b.

_____. "Some Boundary Conditions for a Monotone Analysis of Symmetric Matrices." *Psychometrika* 36 (June): 195-203, 1971.

Lingoes, James C., and E. Roskam. "Minissa-I: A Fortran IV Program for the Smallest Space Analysis of Square Symmetric Matrices." *Behavioral Science* 15: 204-205, 1970.

Lipset, Seymour Martin. *Political Man*. Garden City, N.Y.: Doubleday, 1963.

_____. *Revolution and Counter-revolution*. New York: Basic Books, 1968.

_____. *Politics and the Social Sciences*. New York: Oxford University Press, 1969.

Lipset, Seymour Martin, and Earl Raab. *The Politics of Unreason: Right-Wing Extremism in America*. New York: Harper and Row, 1970.

Luttbeg, Norman R. "The Structure of Beliefs Among Leaders and the Public." *Public Opinion Quarterly* 32 (Fall): 398-409, 1968.

Macrae, Duncan, and James A. Neldrum. "Critical Elections in Illinois: 1888-1958." *American Political Science Review* 54 (September): 669-683, 1960.

May, John D. "Democracy, Party 'Evolution' and Duverger." *Comparative Political Studies* 2 (July): 214-225, 1970.

McClosky, Herbert. "Conservatism and Personality." *American Political Science Review* 52: 27-45, 1958.

_____. "Consensus and Ideology in American Politics." *American Political Science Review* 58 (June): 361-382, 1964.

McClosky, Herbert, Paul J. Hoffman, and Rosemary O'Hara. "Issue Conflict and Consensus Among Party Leaders and Followers." *American Political Science Review* 54 (June): 406-427, 1960.

Merelman, Richard M. "The Development of Political Ideology: A Framework for the Analysis of Political Socialization." *American Political Science Review* 63 (September): 750-767, 1969.

Milbrath, Lester W. *Political Participation*. Chicago: Rand McNally, 1965.

Munsterburg, Hugo. *The Americans*. New York: McClure and Phillips, 1904.

Olsen, Marvin E. "Liberal-Conservative Attitude Crystallization." *Sociological Quarterly* 3 (January): 17-26, 1962.

Reiss, Albert J., Jr. "Crime, Law and Order as Election Issues." *TransAction* 5 (October): 2-4, 1968.

Rice, Stuart A. *Quantitative Methods in Politics*. New York: Knopf, 1928.

Riker, William H. *The Theory of Political Coalitions*. New Haven: Yale University Press, 1967.

Robinson, John P., Jerrold G. Rusk, and Kendra B. Head. "Measures of Political Attitudes." Ann Arbor: Institute for Social Research, The University of Michigan, 1970.

Rokeach, Milton. *The Open and Closed Mind: Investigations into the Nature of Belief Systems and Personality Systems*. New York: Basic Books, 1960.

_____. "The Role of Values in Public Opinion Research." *Public Opinion Quarterly* 32 (Winter): 547-559, 1969a.

_____. *Beliefs, Attitudes, and Values: A Theory of Organization and Change*. San Francisco: Jossey-Bass, 1969b.

_____. "The Measurement of Values and Value Systems." In G. Acarian and J.W. Souele (Eds.) *Social Psychology and Political Behavior*. Columbus, Ohio: Childs Merrill, 1971.

_____. "A Two-Value Model of Politics" (Chapter 6). In *The Nature of Human Values*. New York: Free Press, 1973.

Rokeach, Milton, and Peter Kliejunas. "Behavior as a Function of Attitude-Toward-Object and Attitude-Toward-Situation." *Journal of Personality and Social Psychology* 22 (no. 2): 194-201, 1972.

Rokeach, Milton, and Seymour Parker. "Values as Social Indicators of Poverty and Race Relations in America." *Annals of American Academy of Political and Social Science* 338 (March): 97-111, 1970.

Rokkan, Stein, and Angus Campbell. "Norway and the United States of America." *International Social Science Journal* 12(1): 69-99, 1960.

Rush, Gary B. "Status Inconsistency and Right-Wing Extremism." *American Sociological Review* 32 (February): 86-93, 1967.

Sabine, George. *A History of Political Theory*. New York: Holt, 1963.

Sanai, Mahmoud. "A Factorial Study of Social Attitudes." *Journal of Social Psychology* 31: 167-182, 1950.

Sarnoff, Irving, and Daniel Katz. "The Motivational Bases of Attitude Change." *Journal of Abnormal and Social Psychology* 49: 115-124, 1954.

Sartori, Giovanni. "Politics, Ideology, and Belief Systems." *American Political Science Review* 63 (June): 398-411, 1969.

Scott, James C. *Political Ideology in Malaysia: Reality and the Beliefs of an Elite*. New Haven: Yale University Press, 1968.

Segal, David R. "Partisan Realignment in the United States," *Public Opinion Quarterly* 32 (Fall): 441-444, 1968a.

_____. "A Proposal to Experiment with New Methods of Measuring Partisanship in Social Surveys." Center for Research on Social Organization, The University of Michigan (Mimeo), 1968b.

Segal, David R. "Status Inconsistency, Cross-Pressures and American Political Behavior." *American Sociological Review* 34 (June): 352-359, 1969.

Segal, David R., and Marcus Felson. "Social Status and Family Economic Behavior." In Eleanor Sheldon (Ed.) *Family Life Style and Economic Behavior*. Philadelphia: Lippincott, 1973.

Segal, David R., and Gerald Kent Hikel. "The Spatial Distribution of the Electoral Market." *Working Paper #56*, Center for Research on Social Organization, The University of Michigan, 1970.

Segal, David R., and David Knoke. "Social and Economic Bases of Political Partisanship in the United States." *American Journal of Economics & Sociology* 29 (July): 253-262., 1970.

Segal, David R., and Marshall W. Meyer. "The Social Context of Political Partisanship." In Mattei Dogan and Stein Rokkan (Eds.) *Quantitative Ecological Analysis in the Social Sciences*. Cambridge, Mass.: M.I.T. Press, 1968.

Segal, David R., and Thomas S. Smith. "Congressional Responsibility and the Organization of Constituency Attitudes." *Social Science Quarterly* 51 (December): 743-749, 1970.

Segal, Mady Wechsler. "Selective Processes Operating in the Defense of Consonance." *Psychology* 7 (May): 14-36, 1970.

Sellers, Charles. "The Equilibrium Cycle in Two-Party Politics." *Public Opinion Quarterly* (Winter): 16-38, 1965.

Shapiro, Michael J. "Rational Political Man: A Synthesis of Economic and Social-Psychological Perspectives." *American Political Science Review* 63 (December): 1106-1119, 1969.

Shils, Edward A. "Authoritarianism: 'Right' and 'Left' " (pp. 24-49). In R. Christie and M. Jahoda (Eds.) *Studies in the Scope and Method of "The Authoritarian Personality."* Glencoe, Ill.: Free Press, 1954.

Smithies, Arthur. "Optimum Location in Spatial Competition." *Journal of Political Economy* 49: 423-457, 1941.

Stokes, Donald E. "Spatial Model of Party Competition" (pp. 161-179). In Angus Campbell, Philip E. Converse, Warren E. Miller, and Donald E. Stokes *Elections and the Political Order*. New York: John Wiley, 1966.

Stokes, Donald E., and Warren E. Miller. "Party Government and the Saliency of Congress." *Public Opinion Quarterly* 26 (Winter): 534-546, 1962.

Survey Research Center. "The Distribution of Party Identification in the United States." The University of Michigan, 1968.

_____. *Technical Report*. University of Michigan, 1969.

Valen, Henry, and Daniel Katz. Political Parties in Norway: A Community Study: Oslo, Norway, Universitets for Laget, 1964.

Wilker, Harry R., and Lester W. Milbrath. "Political Belief Systems and Political Behavior." *Social Science Quarterly* 51 (December): 477-493, 1970.

Wolfe, Arthur C. "Some Results of the 1966-67 Election Study." Survey Research Center, University of Michigan (Memorandum), 1967.

Wolfe, Arthur C. "Challenge from the Right: The Basis of Voter Support for Wallace in 1968." Survey Research Center, The University of Michigan, 1969.

# Index

# Index

147

## About the Author

**Gerald Kent Hikel** took an Honours B.A. at McGill University in 1968 and the M.A. in 1969 at the University of Michigan, where he also received the Ph.D in Social Organization in 1971. His current literary projects include the editing of *Political Values,* and the examination with Albert J. Reiss, Jr. of *Discretionary Changes in Prosecutorial Decision-Making.* Dr. Hikel has been affiliated with Yale University's Institution for Social and Policy Studies as Research Sociologist since 1971.